Language, Schools, and Government in Cameroon
HUGH O. H. VERNON-JACKSON

Divergence in Educational Development:
the Case of Kenya and Uganda
SHELDON G. WEEKS

Political Socialization in the New Nations of Africa
PENELOPE ROACH

Educating the Bureaucracy in a New Polity
TAMAR GOLAN

"Education for Self-Reliance" in Tanzania
(A Study of Its Vocational Aspects)
WILLIAM A. DODD

The Development of Education in East Africa
JOHN CAMERON

The Cost of Learning
LOUIS COWAN

Traditional Ethiopian Church Education
ALAKA I. KA

D1287744

Children in Africa:

A Review of Psychological Research

JUDITH L. EVANS

Center for Education in Africa
Institute of International Studies
Teachers College, Columbia University

TEACHERS COLLEGE PRESS

Teachers College, Columbia University
New York, New York

Manufactured in the United States of America

Dedicated to David

Contents

Introduction

The world is like the play of children, the one in front often becomes the one behind.

Hausa Proverb

Africa, the dark unknown continent, is no longer dark and unknown. Man's knowledge of Africa and its people continues to expand. From primitive global descriptions of Africa our understanding has been increased to the point where we can talk intelligently about specific areas within Africa and discuss them in relatively sophisticated anthropological, economical, and political terms. However, our knowledge of psychological and educational development within African cultures is far more limited. There is an increasing awareness of this paucity, and attempts are being made to expand knowledge in these areas. This book arises out of a need to provide those who are interested in pursuing psychological and educational studies in Africa with a synthesis of our current understanding of the African child.

Presented in this psychological review is a collection of works which provide an overview of the research done with children in Africa from 1900 to 1969. In selecting the references to be included, an attempt was made to achieve a balance between important sources which are not easily obtained and materials which are generally available.

The review is divided into seven chapters. The first deals with philosophical analyses of the African mind, and includes various interpretations of African belief systems. Chapter II deals with intelligence. For the most part it includes references on work done to test the intellectual potential of Africans. The third chapter presents selected studies on the physiological growth of the African child as it relates to his cognitive growth. Chapter IV presents material on the socialization process and is divided into four parts: (1) child-rearing practices; (2) education (formal and informal, traditional and modern); (3) the effects of socialization on personality development; and (4) the acculturation process. Chapters V and VI deal with cognitive development. Chapter V presents material relating to perceptual cognition, and Chapter VI contains references on other areas of cognitive functioning which have been studied in Africa. Chapter VII includes a review of bibliographies on Africa that provides further references for the reader. Works which discuss research methodology in Africa and references to current and proposed research with children in Africa are also included in the last chapter.

1

In general, each chapter has been organized chronologically to give the reader an idea of the progression of ideas and interests over the years. This book presents the viewpoint of the authors whose works are being reviewed and, where critiqued by contemporary and later authors, from their standpoints. In several places questions have been raised about the research methodology employed. The word "African" has been used as it is used in the article being discussed. Therefore, the term is not used uniformly throughout. References to specific tribes are made where authors make these distinctions.

At the end of each chapter is a bibliography which includes the material referred to in that chapter plus additional references on the same subject. Some overlapping of references occurs as articles often contain subject matter discussed in more than one chapter.

It is hoped that this review will serve to show the inadequacies of our present knowledge of the African child, and will provide guidelines for areas of further research.

I. A Philosophical Approach to the African Mind

> The discursive operations of our rational
> thought... require the existence and the employment
> of much that is intricate, in the form of categories,
> concepts, and abstract terms.... They imply an en-
> semble of conditions which we do not find existing
> anywhere in social aggregates of a primitive type.
>
> Lucien Lévy-Bruhl, 1926, p. 105

> The man who is full of trite sayings rejoices in a discussion; it is
> not impossible that the man who answers may silence him.
>
> Hausa Proverb

Explorers, traders, and missionaries who penetrated the African continent in the 1800s recorded, for themselves and interested readers, their impressions of the African peoples. Initially, Africans were described in terms of their physical features, their modes of dress, the physical environments in which they lived, and their daily living patterns. Journals and articles occasionally contained comments on the philosophical thought systems of the African. However, it was not until the 1920s that Lucien Lévy-Bruhl, philosopher, pulled together materials written about Africans in all parts of Africa and attempted to fully describe the thought processes of the "African" (1923, 1926, 1928). His works became the foundation of later articles, both for those who supported and for those who disputed his position.

The term Lévy-Bruhl used to describe primitive modes of thought was "prelogical mentality." He viewed thought processes as a continuum, with the prelogical characteristics of primitive thought as an earlier stage of development. The term *prelogical* is used to describe a rationale that is dependent on memory rather than on logical activity (1926, p. 110). This rationale is a product of the social milieu surrounding the primitive, and is characterized by mysticism and collective representations regulated by the "law of participation" (p. 76). Within primitive society, Lévy-Bruhl noted, the "individual unconsciousness of every member of the group is and remains strictly solidary with the collective consciousness" (p. 365).

Lévy-Bruhl equated Western thought with a position farther along the continuum. The Western social milieu produces an individual who has become clearly differentiated from the group, conscious of himself as a person, and

3

aware of objects and beings outside himself. While Western thought today contains evidence of prelogical processes, it is fundamentally logical.

R. F. Alfred Hoernlé (1927) wrote an article which disputed Lévy-Bruhl's use of the word "prelogical." Hoernlé suggested that a better term would be "prescientific" since the native works logically *within his own frame of reference*. While logical, these primitive thought processes may be difficult for Western man to follow, just as the African has difficulty following the thoughts of the European.

Hoernlé's main thesis was that the difference between Westerner and African is a matter of social heritage rather than of inherent ability. He further maintained that differences are a result of the way the individual is trained and learns to use his mental powers (p. 54).

Franz Boas (1939) disputed the concept of cultural evolution, or, as Lévy-Bruhl termed it, "parallelism of cultural development." Boas showed that all cultures do not go through the same stages of development, but can learn from each other. In discussing the qualities of African thinking, he took the position that African thought processes are "different," but that the reason is due to the environment. Through the centuries, Boas maintained, the environment has produced physiological changes and has also affected the mind, since the mind, rather than the body, is most subject to change (1939, p. 65).

According to Boas the logic of primitive tribes results from the character of knowledge accumulated by previous generations. While Western thought is based on years of experimentation, primitive thought is based on the "crude experience of generations" (p. 238). Boas believed that "the differences between different types of man are, on the whole, small as compared to the range of variation in each type" (p. 94).

Several years earlier, Otto Klineberg (1935) suggested many of the ideas expressed by Boas. Klineberg's book contained an extensive bibliography of all work done in the field of race differences up to that time. After reviewing these works, Klineberg concluded: "Culture can produce and maintain profound differences even in those reactions which psychologists have usually regarded as basic to all behavior . . . " (p. 273). Klineberg reminded the reader that physiological differences have been found, but as yet no one has answered the question of how and if these relate to psychological development. To Klineberg, the important comparisons are not between the primitive and civilized, but between one culture and another.

During the same year, a book by Vernon Brelsford (1935) presented another view on the philosophy of primitive tribes. After reviewing earlier theories of "savage mentality," Brelsford concluded that the different philosophies of life in primitive societies are not a result of any peculiar mental process of function, since the African mind functions in the same way as the Western mind. Instead, different thought systems are the results of customs and traditions produced by and perpetuating the existing social and political system. In an analysis of African philosophy, Brelsford showed that the African sees himself as part of a total system which includes other individuals as well as spirits and things, and he accepts the universe rather than challenging it. The mind is molded by its surroundings; the surroundings are not changed by the individual.

In his book, Brelsford noted that Western modes of thought were being imposed on the African, and he predicted that this would continue – a phenomenon which he felt would be detrimental to the existing culture. Brelsford concluded by saying that Western man has tended to see the African as inferior, but "the more means we have of studying [the African] the more sense and reason do we find" (p. 49).

S. D. Porteus (1937) felt that not enough was known about primitive man to conclude that differences were largely due to environment, as suggested by Klineberg and Brelsford before, and Boas later. After comparing the Aborigines of Central Australia with the Bushmen of South Africa, Porteus concluded that there are racial differences in mentality, and that it is not unreasonable to expect this when one takes into consideration the various conditions to which man must adjust (p. 213).

Porteus advocated the use of Western tests on peoples of other cultures since the results provide information on whether the native has the skills necessary to adjust to Western society, irrespective of whether these tests tap innate abilities. He recognized the difficulties of administering tests to a non-Western culture, and emphasized that characteristics of the culture should be taken into consideration when looking at results (p. 225).

Later authors have suggested that in order to understand African thought processes a different approach should be taken. Godfrey Lienhardt (1954) suggested that in order to understand what totems, expressions, rituals, and experiences mean to a society, Western man must make the same assumptions that the society under study does. To illustrate the understandings that can be gained by this approach, Lienhardt gave several examples of how the thinking and actions accompanying witchcraft are consistent with the underlying assumptions of the culture.

Meyer Fortes (1954) emphasized the role of the existing culture in producing a society's philosophical system. Man is made a part of his culture through a social context. Culture comes to man from outside himself and, while internalized by the individual, is dependent in form on what exists externally. Through a knowledge of the culture it is possible to understand the use of such quantities as time and space and other systems of thought.

Placide Tempels (1959) believed that to understand a people such as the Bantu, one must be familiar with the metaphysical foundations of their culture. From his analysis of Bantu philosophy, Tempels showed how it is possible to understand a people once one recognizes and respects their

6

cultural heritage. Tempels' work is an example of the type of insight which can result when an author has respect for the individuals with whom he is working.

The most recent attempt at a philosophical analysis of primitive cultures is provided by Claude Lévi-Strauss (1966). The author presents a new look at some of the phenomena found in primitive cultures that were described by Lévy-Bruhl and others. Lévi-Strauss showed how ethnographic data is often inadequate because it is limited in its approach and does not lend itself to wider analysis. Only with an intimate knowledge of the particular society is one able to find the logic in its system of thought.

To illustrate the insight which can be gained through an in-depth study of a culture, Lévi-Strauss discusses the development of classification systems within several societies. In the author's first description of categories of classification the dimensions noted appear arbitrary. The system becomes a coherent whole only when the author presents the society as a totality. He also illustrates how words chosen to designate classes have no intrinsic significance. "Their meaning is one of 'position' – a function of the history and cultural context on the one hand and of the structural system in which they are called upon to appear on the other" (p. 55).

Lévi-Strauss' discussion makes it readily apparent that Western assumptions about classification are the result of our world view and not the result of intrinsic classes. Only with an understanding of the total society can hypotheses be developed about the thought processes encouraged by a culture. It is from this vantage point that research should begin, rather than assuming that systems of thought are analogous across the world's societies.

From the literature discussed above it is possible to follow the change in emphasis through time. Early philosophers attempted to understand African thought systems by collecting comments from untrained observers and creating a philosophical structure based on Western constructs. The resultant structure was then applied to all African peoples south of the Sahara. Through time, increased knowledge of the African continent has revealed its diversity and shown the folly of applying a specific philosophical system to all Africans. More recent works indicate an attempt to base philosophical analyses on a study of the total society.

BIBLIOGRAPHY

Anastasi, Anne, and Foley, John. *Differential Psychology: Individual and Group Differences in Behavior.* New York: Macmillan, 1949.

Boas, Franz. *The Mind of Primitive Man.* New York: Macmillan, 1939.

Brelsford, Vernon. *Primitive Philosophy.* London: John Balse, Sons & Danielson, Ltd., 1935.

Denis, F. "L'Enseignement Traditionnel au Congo avant l'Arrivée des Blancs." *La Revue Nouvelle,* 1951, *13*(4), pp. 346-355.

Doob, Leonard. *Becoming More Civilized: A Psychological Exploration.* New Haven: Yale University Press, 1960.

Fortes, Meyer. "Mind," in E. E. Evans-Pritchard, *et al. The Institutions of Primitive Society.* Oxford: Blackwell, 1954, pp. 81-94.

————, and Dieterlen, G. (eds.). *African Systems of Thought.* London: Oxford University Press, 1965.

Frantz, Charles. "The African Personality: Myth and Reality." *Journal of Human Relations,* 1969, *8,* pp. 455-464.

Garth, T. R. *Race Psychology: A Study of Racial Mental Differences.* New York: McGraw-Hill, 1931.

Hoernlé, R. F. Alfred. "Study of the Black Man's Mind." *Journal of Philosophical Studies,* 1927, *2*(5), pp. 52-61.

Klineberg, Otto. *Race Differences.* New York: Harper & Bros., 1935.

Lévi-Strauss, Claude. *The Savage Mind.* London: Weidenfeld & Nicolson, 1966.

Lévy-Bruhl, Lucien. *Primitive Mentality.* London: Allen & Unwin, 1923.

————. *How Natives Think.* London: Allen & Unwin, 1926.

————. *The "Soul" of the Primitive.* London: Allen & Unwin, 1928.

Lienhardt, Godfrey. "Modes of Thought," in E. E. Evans-Pritchard, *et al. The Institutions of Primitive Society.* Oxford: Blackwell, 1954, pp. 95-107.

Nadel, S. F. "A Field Experiment in Racial Psychology." *British Journal of Psychology,* 1947, *28*(2), pp. 195-211.

Porteus, S. D. *The Psychology of Primitive People.* London: E. Arnold, 1931.

————. *Primitive Intelligence and Environment.* New York: Macmillan, 1937.

Radin, Paul. *The World of Primitive Man.* New York: Henry Schuman, 1953.

Ritchie, J. F. *The African as Suckling and as Adult (A Psychological Study).* Rhodes-Livingstone Institute, Northern Rhodesia. Paper No. 9, 1943.

————. "The African as Grown-up Nursling." *Rhodes-Livingstone Journal,* 1944, *1,* pp. 55-60.

Tempels, Placide. *Bantu Philosophy.* Paris: Présence Africaine, 1959.

Van der Post, Laurens. *The Lost World of the Kalahari.* London: Hogarth Press, 1958.

Verhaegen, Paul. "Study of the African Personality in the Belgian Congo," in Report of the CSA Meeting of Specialists on the Basic Psychological Structures of African and Madagascan Populations; Commission for Technical Cooperation in Africa South of the Sahara. *Scientific Council for Africa South of the Sahara,* Publication No. 51, 1959.

Vernon, P. E. "Race and Intelligence." *Eugenics Review,* 1959, *51,* pp. 99-101.

Vilikazi, A. "Changing Concepts of the Self and the Supernatural in Africa." *Annals of the New York Academy of Sciences,* 1962, *96,* pp. 670-675.

II. Intelligence

I rather imagine that in his own tribal ways, foresight and planning are not of much value to the ordinary man: but considering the direction of the acculturation process the question as to who is the most intelligent by native standards is beside the mark.

S. D. Porteus, 1937, p. 258

We speak by proverbs: he who is intelligent will understand.
Kikuyu Proverb

The greatest concentration of research done with African children is in the realm of intelligence assessment. Throughout this discussion on intelligence testing, it is important to keep in mind both the cultural background of the investigator and the general level of knowledge about intelligence testing which existed in Western cultures during comparable time periods.

In the early 1900s work was done in South Africa in an attempt to ascertain the educational potential of Africans. In 1915 and 1916 C. T. Loram gave a series of mental tests to natives, Asians, and Europeans in South Africa. He found that the native was "markedly inferior" to both the Asian and the European. While natives scored lower than Asians, he ruled out language as having a significant effect, since English was a second language for both. Loram felt that the inferiority was not necessarily a permanent disability, and that by using "selective breeding" the educational potential of the native could be raised (1917).

H. R. Loades and S. G. Rich (1917) translated the standard Binet test, "changing some specific items which were not appropriate," and administered the test to educated natives — both children and adults. Stated Loades and Rich: "Our results indicate that post-pubertal development of the mind is different in Natives from what it is in Europeans" (p. 383). The authors were also interested in giving their tests to uneducated natives to "show to what extent it is true that without education the mind of the Native ceases to develop after puberty, and to what extent education prevents this" (p. 380). There were no further references to indicate if this study was carried out.

In 1927 T. M. H. Endemann did a study of the quality and determinants of African intelligence. He reached the general conclusion that the native is unable to form abstract concepts, and that he has difficulty with such subjects as mathematics and science, as he does not have an understanding of the concepts involved.

9

It should be noted that these studies were done by administering Western-developed tests to Africans. Generally, the tests were administered in the same way they would be to European children, and results were looked at in terms of how the African subjects compared with the norms established in Western cultures. It is no wonder the African was seen as "inferior." The trend in the late 1920s was to hypothesize about the causes of Africans' poor test results.

M. Lawrence Fick (1929) suggested some of the conditions that might help to explain Africans' performances on individual tests: their inexperience with materials presented pictorially in tasks; the existence of a teaching system which fosters reliance on memory work; and the problem of language, in that the tests were administered in English. Although Fick raised some important questions, his experiments did not control adequately for any of the factors he felt affected results.

In a later experiment, Fick (1939a) attempted to control the environment. In order to do this he compared "good" natives with poor white Afrikaners. The Afrikaners had little educational opportunity and came from an "inferior environment." When the natives still scored lower, Fick concluded that the difference was the result of innate inferiority rather than of environmental effects, and that the inferiority was not a temporary phenomenon (p. 52, p. 56). According to Fick, the inferiority "limits considerably the proportion of Natives who can benefit by education of the ordinary type beyond the rudimentary" (p. 56). It is interesting to note that only in one anlaysis by Fick was any consideration made of the cultural characteristics of the tribes involved.

In the same paper, Fick reviewed all the intelligence testing which had so far occurred in South Africa with Africans and concluded: "All objective and scientific estimates of the educability of the Natives . . . indicate a marked inferiority on the part of the Native in comparison with European pupils of the same age" (p. 51).

Fick's work was strongly criticized by later authors and contemporaries who supported an environmentalist theory, rather than an inheritance theory as an explanation of tested differences. One critic was J. M. Winterbottom (1948) who summarized Fick's work as follows:

Fick took a sample of the South African Bantu about the composition of which the only things certain are that it was inadequate in number and unrepresentative; . . . he tested the member's intelligence by means of tests . . . unsuitable in character without making allowances for their unsuitability . . . and the conclusions drawn from the data he assembled were unjustifiable and frequently demonstrably wrong (p. 57).

Besides Fick, other writers of the 1930s were also looking at the environmental factors which appeared to affect performance on intelligence tests. J. A. Jansen VanRensburg (1938) in South Africa controlled for seven factors in his testing: (1) obtaining a representative sample of subjects in native and white groups; (2) language; (3) the type of test that would be most appropriate: (4) the customs and attitudes toward tests which might influence the speed and achievement motivation of the subject; (5) the attitude of the subject toward the tester; (6) the educational level of the subject; and (7) the social and economic conditions of the groups selected. VanRensburg administered three types of tests to a group of Europeans and to a group of Africans. The results of these tests indicated that the South African native, "has not the learning ability to be able to compete on equal terms with the Average European except in tasks of an extremely simple nature . . . and that the difference in ability is partly innate" (p. 43).

The above authors worked with Africans in South Africa, and while their results may be significant related to the social policy being developed, interpretation of test results in South Africa may more accurately reflect the general acceptance of intelligence tests throughout Western cultures as an adequate measure of innate ability. During this same time work was being done in only a few other parts of Africa.

One psychologist working outside South Africa was Richard Oliver, whose work was done in East Africa. More interested in looking at African intelligence in terms of what it can practically reveal for education rather than for its scientific implications about the ability of races, Oliver (1932a) administered a test which was non-verbal in response. With this he hoped to overcome language problems. However, the test did not satisfy him since it was still verbal in presentation. Oliver has been criticized because he did not adequately follow up or standardized the General Intelligence Test which he devised (Winterbottom, 1948; Scott, 1950).

Other studies done by Oliver in East Africa indicated that the African was behind the European in some skills (1933a, 1933b, 1933c). However, his results did not show the African to be as far behind the European as the results from South Africa indicated. Oliver emphasized the fact that among Africans, as among Europeans, there is a wide range of ability.

A study by H. W. Nissen, S. Machover and Elaine Kinder (1935) attempted to look at the immediately present abilities of children between the ages of five and fourteen in the SouSou tribe. The authors administered a series of twelve tests – each requiring a different skill – to every subject (50Ss). In their article they included an ethnographic sketch of the tribe and used this as a frame of reference for interpreting the data.

The authors stated that the results indicated that both racial and environmental factors are relevant to a child's performance on these tests. They also pointed out that intelligence is a culturally defined phenomenon influenced by what is valued in Western society, Western culture having a different "cultural set" from African societies. The role of the cultural set of a people is to condition the "development of functions with consequent cumulative differentiation" (p. 315). Thus, they concluded that it is unrealistic to expect that a test devised in the Western cultural set is validly transferable to another culture.

This view was shared by Simon Biesheuvel (1943) and expressed in his book *African Intelligence*. In it Biesheuvel discussed the use of Western tests with Africans and the difficulties involved in trying to compare the intelligence of whites and Africans. *African Intelligence* was the forerunner of a series of articles by Biesheuvel, who was basically an environmentalist in his approach to the problem of tested differences. Some of the factors Biesheuvel discussed as causing variance are: the influence of the cultural milieu; the effect of the home environment on the urban and rural African; the level of education he is receiving; and the effect of nutrition on his mental and physical development.

A strong supporter of Biesheuvel, Winterbottom (1948) expounded on the importance of *African Intelligence*. He also discussed the reason for and the history of the development of intelligence tests, and emphasized that the materials used in intelligence tests must be based on the normal environment of the people to be tested (p. 55). For this reason a test devised for one culture cannot be expected to apply to another.

Winterbottom raised two important issues. First, little is known about the inheritance of intelligence and the effects of the environment on inherited ability. Second, inter-racial comparisons can be highly emotionally charged, and researchers who approach their work with a bias can consciously or unconsciously direct the research in such a way as to find the results they are seeking in their data.

Besides taking a look at the environment and hypothesizing about its effect on test scores, psychologists were beginning to realize that perhaps the tests they were using were inappropriate in the African context. Energy was next directed toward adapting Western tests so that they would be more culturally relevant. As will be shown by the discussion which follows, during the 1950s psychologists and educationalists throughout Africa were so involved. This was accomplished with varying degrees of success.

J. D. Clarke (1948) saw language as one of the problems of test adaptation. Therefore, he administered a set of Binet tests which required only a "minimum linguistic knowledge."* In his article Clarke discussed the materials, procedures, and scores for each test used and their potential use with Africans.

---

*Generally, the scores were still somewhat lower than standardized Western scores, however, the Africans did better on these tests than on those which rely strongly on verbal skills.

Bernard Notcutt (1949) administered Raven's Progressive Matrices, a non-verbal intelligence test, to Zulus, and concluded that the statistical distribution for Zulus and Europeans was quite different; the distribution of scores for Zulus was positively skewed, for Europeans it was negatively skewed. Thus, it was not possible to compare scores across groups. He also found that Raven's Progressive Matrices was suitable neither for making inferences about the "true" distribution of African abilities nor their "real" rate of growth (p. 70).

In a later article, Notcutt (1950) discussed five tests which he felt had been adequately standardized for use with native school children in South Africa. They were: the Goodenough Draw-A-Man Test; Raven's Progressive Matrices (although he had previously found this test inadequate); a Zulu Vocabulary Test; an adaptation of the Knox Cube Test (Span of Apprehension); and an adaptation of the Kohs Block Test (Cube Pattern Test). Notcutt indicated that the testability of subjects is culturally determined, and that not all people are suitable subjects. In order to be accurately tested, subjects must be familiar with and accept "Western bureaucratic procedures" (p. 195).

In the Sudan, G. C. Scott's (1950) first attempt to test Africans was unsuccessful. He found that the translation of foreign verbal tests with "a priori" adaptations were invalid and unreliable. He then devised his own test which he based on two principles. First, items used should be wholly suited to the child's environment. Second, presentation of items must suit the environment. In other words, the child must understand what he is asked to do. The tests Scott developed were only provisional and the sampling was limited, so adequate standardizations were not acquired.

G. R. Dent (1949) examined the applicability of a test devised in Africa – The South African Group Intelligence Test, developed by R. W. Wilrocks. Dent analyzed the test and concluded that cultural characteristics of the Zulus were not taken into consideration when the test was devised. For example, Zulus are not time conscious and do not work for speed, yet results of the test are partially interpreted on the basis of how long the subject took to complete it. Also, Zulus answer only questions they are sure they know the answers to, rather than making a guess. Althought the test is administered in Zulu, it is unsuitable because it is basically European in construction and presumes an analytic mode of verbal thought. Dent also discussed the effects of environment on test performance: "Growth of ability occurs from without rather than from within, in that it is dependent upon the contacts provided by the outside world" (p. 40).

Robert Maistriaux (1955, 1956) began his work by making observations of the mental level of Africans. He then introduced a series of tests, discussed at some length in his second article, which were given to Africans in the Belgian Congo. His results led him to the conclusion that:

there is no qualitative difference between the intelligence of Negroes and that of Whites, but, generally speaking, the Central African Negroes are quantitatively much less successful than White people when it comes to any test requiring abstract intelligence (p. 25).

Maistriaux continued his article with a discussion of the causes of and possible remedies for the underdevelopment found in the Belgian Congo. As a means of speeding up the evolution of Africans, he advocated the education of indigenous women and a review of syllabuses and teaching methods in the light of the actual aptitudes of the pupils.

V. King (1957), working in Sierra Leone, looked at the results of an intelligence test administered to Africans there. He concluded that the test gave an indication of a general retardation of the population. This King attributed to two features in the environment: the illiteracy of adults, and the low teaching standards found in the schools.

One aspect of the African's attitude that affects his test score is his lack of concern for completing a task within a prescribed time. André Ombredane, Paul Bertelson, and Elaine Beniest-Noirot (1958) were interested in seeing if this was related to task difficulty. A group of African adult males and one of Belgian adult males were given a task to complete and were timed on their performance. When the two groups were finished, each African was matched for accuracy with a Belgian. Their times were then compared. The authors concluded that, as far as these tasks were concerned, the slowness of the African was not related to task difficulty. Slowness is "more easily explained by a general lack of interest in speed performance rather than by a slower operation of mental functions" (p. 336). John McFie's (1961) work indicated that when trained to work for speed this difficulty is overcome.

Simone Fridjhon (1961) used the PACTO Test with South Africans since she felt it tested "some type of basic intelligence" (p. 185). Results indicated the same hierarchy of test scores as other intelligence tests used with Africans, but suggested several things to Fridjhon. First, there was a different order of item difficulty within the various sampling groups. In other words, the complexity of the test items is not as easily determined as previously thought. Second, although Fridjhon believed that symmetry is pleasing to everyone, she did raise the question of whether personal preference plays a part in the choices made by the subjects. This led to a further question: To what extent are preferences for various types of designs determined by the culture?

During the late 1950s and 1960s, there was an increased interest in research on intelligence. For this reason, the following section will not present articles chronologically, but according to specific areas of research.

INTELLIGENCE: INHERENT ABILITY OR EDUCATION?

After spending many years attempting to test the "intelligence" of the African, psychologists began asking what Western tests were really testing in the African setting. The basic question asked was: Are the tests tapping the innate ability of the children, their educational level, or their cultural heritage? One tentative answer to the question suggested that it was the child's cultural milieu that was being tested.

In an attempt to look at the influence of subtle differences in cultures Biesheuvel did an experiment with Renée Liddicoat (1959), in which they compared Afrikaners and English culture groups in South Africa. By using these groups the authors hoped to control for the genetic factor as closely as possible. Their sample was extensive and controlled for socio-economic level and education. In four of the five socio-economic groups, the English scored higher than the Afrikaners. This difference is explained by the authors as the result of the greater simplicity and lower stimulation level of the Afrikaners' language. The fact that there was no significant difference between the lowest socio-economic groups is explained by the fact that, at this level, the general stimulation of the English is too low and undifferentiated to show a cultural difference. From this comparison the authors concluded: "The study has demonstrated that the subtle differences that occur within a national culture can have a measurable effect both on intelligence test performance and on development of intellectual potentialities as such" (p. 13).

While Biesheuvel felt that culture was a significant factor in test performance, he did not feel that all other factors could be categorically excluded. This feeling was echoed by H. J. Rosseau (1962) who summed up his feelings as follows:

> In every field of human endeavor cultural differences pervade performance ... [however] between different families of the human race innate differences of general and specific ability may quite possibly exist: no one can tell (p. 336).

Thus, psychologists acknowledged the effect of culture on test results, but not being totally satisfied continued to look for other factors which might also influence performance. One area explored was the possible effects of formal education, in the Western sense, on children's test scores.

An example of the influence of education on tested ability can be found in the work of McFie (1954, 1961). In the early study, his results suggested that the difference between the African and European in ability on a constructional test—the African scoring lower—was due to the African's lack of education. He tested this hypothesis by doing a longitudinal study with African boys entering technical school. These boys were given a series of verbal, numerical, pictorial, construction, abstract, and memory for designs tests. The scores on the non-language tests were low and indicated that the subjects' orientations of drawn and constructed figures were inaccurate. After two years of technical training they were retested, and it was found that there was a significant increase in their speed and accuracy of orientation, and a more "synthetic" approach to visual material (1961). McFie attributed this growth to the experience the boys had with tasks specifically related to perceptual orientation.

Ombredane, whose work was done in the Belgian Congo, placed greater emphasis on knowing at what level the African child was intellectually, rather than on making comparisons with a Western counterpart. He was also interested in trying to discover children's modes of thinking. In a discussion of the then current use of different intelligence tests, Ombredane questioned whether one could separate the intellectual level of a child from his educational level. Ombredane felt that the results of intelligence tests tended to show the general acculturation level of the child, rather than intellectual potential. While an idea of the acculturation level can help to predict how well the individual will fit into the model that Western society has imposed, it does not give a picture of innate ability. J. M. Faverage and J. C. Falmagne have noted that Ombredane emphasized the importance of knowledge of the traditional heritage, "for that part of culture which enters into the operations called intellectual, appears to be much larger than we would have ordinarily supposed" (1962, p. 31).

P. Vernon (1959) emphasized that the degree to which a child's potential was developed depended to a large extent on the stimulus he received. However, Vernon, unlike many of his contemporaries, felt that the use of Western tests in non-Western cultures is feasible, for although it does not provide an indication of innate ability, the results are relevant in terms of the future educational and vocational pursuits of the individual. Western tests reveal a kind of intelligence based on the ability to comprehend, reason, learn, and judge effectively in school. These abilities he said, "although based fundamentally on innate brain potentiality, only develop insofar as they are stimulated by upbringing and they develop very differently with different kinds and amounts of stimulus" (p. 101).

The main forces on intellectual development, as described by Vernon, are: the physical factors of health and nutrition; perceptual deprivation; lack of sufficient numbers of schools and continuity and quality of schooling; linguistic difficulties; emotional factors in the home; the values and principles underlying the society; and the unfamiliarity of peoples in developing countries with tests (1966, p. 6).

Vernon was also very interested in studying the environmental forces which have the greatest impact on intellectual development, and then manipulating these factors for greater intellectual growth. Vernon's work contains recommendations for educationalists as to how they can raise the standards of education in developing countries and encourage greater intellectual growth.

TESTS FOR PREDICTION

In the 1960s several individuals connected with the then University College of Rhodesia and Nyasaland became interested in devising tests for Africans which could be used for the purposes of school selection at the end of primary school. R. MacArthur, Sidney Irvine, and Arthur Brimble (1964) undertook an extensive survey of the mental abilities of Africans in Rhodesia and Nyasaland. The purpose of their study was to devise better tests to help make the right judgments about where children fit into the educational system. Their survey provided some indication of the type of child who will be most successful in the African secondary schools which are based on Western educational models.

Jonathan Silvey (1964) expressed a concern about the tests which were being used in various parts of Africa for selection at the end of primary school. Silvey recognized that one difficulty in devising tests is having a working definition of intelligence on which to base the test. Since psychologists have not proved the universality of Western psychological constructs, a Western definition of intelligence may not be meaningful in another society. Silvey felt "there are few skills, common to every culture, which are sufficiently *overlearnt* to be suitable as the basis for measures which are valid between cultures and which discriminate within cultures" (p. 11). He also pointed out that using ability tests for educational prediction is unlikely to tap innate intelligence, but rather is a test of previous education and experience. "The essential test of tests in Africa should be their predictive validity not their construct or content validities" (p. 21).

Brimble (1964) devised a test of pictorial recognition and administered it to more than 700 children in Standard V in the Lusaka area. After analyzing the results, Brimble concluded that it is possible to construct an ability test for Africans by using the same procedures one would use in the Western world. Also, his test correlated positively with the school assessment of the child, which was based on a uniform external examination (p. 33). Brimble stated that his test can be used to predict success in the upper primary schools and for selection purposes at other levels.

Through the work done by Irvine (1963a, b), knowledge has been gained about the use of various tests within the school population. Irvine's work was based on the theoretical framework that mental abilities are environmentally relative, if genetically finite. He felt that psychologically constructed tests could be used for predictive purposes if the subjects were literate in English.

Of the three tests he felt were worthwhile, two were devised at the National Institute of Personnel Research, Johannesburg – the Spiral Nines Test and the Mental Alertness Test. The third was Raven's Progressive Matrices. While the trend in testing Africans has been to use the results for descriptive purposes, Irvine felt that verbal and non-verbal tests should be based on local norms and standardized with African groups in order to have valid predictive and evaluative meanings (1963a, p. 49).

Irvine was particularly interested in the child at the end of primary education. Some of the results of his testing show that: (1) the older the child is when he enters school, the less likely he is to have high test scores at the end of his primary education; (2) repeaters perform poorly on tests – to have a child repeat a grade is poor economy and does not add to the education of the child; (3) boys score consistently higher than girls – in their society boys are encouraged to be dominant and use their English more; and (4) the number of years resident in an urban area correlates positively with high test scores (1962). Irvine felt that the most valid assessment of a child at the end of primary schooling is gained through using a combination of psychologically based tests, headmaster's estimates, and tests of verbal and non-verbal intelligence (1954).

P. A. Swarz (1963) discussed the necessity of developing selection tests applicable to the African educational context and the country's future manpower needs. He felt attention should be directed toward adequately steering children to technical and vocation occupations, as well as preparing them for further academic studies. Swarz developed a paper and pencil test to be used for selection purposes in Northern Nigeria. He concluded his article with a discussion of research methodology peculiar to the African setting, and proposed a systematic procedure for the design of research related to test adaptation. Swarz's work is an example of a trend to devise tests within and specifically for Africa.

This chapter continues with several references to work recently attempted along these lines, and concludes with a discussion of research methodology in Africa.

THE DEVELOPMENT OF CULTURALLY RELEVANT TESTS

A. E. G. Pillner (1964) worked with educators in West Africa to devise a set of tests to be used with children entering school. He found that teachers' evaluations alone were not useful, since teachers could not be entirely objective and did, in fact, vary in their standards. Pillner used various test items with West African children and found "their responses were remarkably similar to those obtained from children in Great Britain," in spite of the fact that English is a second language to them (p. 5). Pillner hoped that his work would help to provide guidelines for further test development.

Douglass Price-Williams (1961), in an attempt to lay groundwork for the development of an intelligence test for Nigeria, administered a Compound Series Test (Test i) of the Differential Test Battery, by J. R. Morrisby, to a group from the Tiv tribe, and found that the test did separate the bright from the dull child. In his analysis of the results, Price-Williams took into consideration various attributes of the Tiv culture which might affect test scores. However, he emphasized that this was only an experimental attempt. To devise an adequate intelligence test for Nigeria requires further work.

E. T. Abiola (1965) was also interested in studying the nature of intellectual development in the African child. He attempted to get at this by trying to understand the development of the patterns of abilities within particular cultural groups. For his study, Abiola used two groups of Yoruba children at each age level from one to five. One group had educated mothers, the other mothers who were strongly traditional. Abiola described in detail the methods used and the results obtained. He found that the most significant factor affecting intellectual growth in both groups was the maturation level of the child. He concluded his article with a set of questions, the answers to which he felt were important in order to better understand the African child:

1. What are the relevant environmental factors affecting perceptual and conceptual development, and how do these factors relate to intellectual development?
2. How do intellectual and perceptual abilities develop after the age of five?
3. Are the quantitative, qualitative, and developmental disparities between the groups temporary or permanent? What effects do such disparities have on subsequent intellectual development of the child?
4. Is the disparity between maturation and learning a general one? What effects does such disparity have on subsequent intellectual development and performance?
5. What are the permanent effects of the divergent systems of child rearing on the emotional life of the child, and how do these affect the intellectual life of the child? (pp. 37-58)

METHODOLOGY

Paul Verhaegen and J. L. Laroche (1958) were concerned with the problems of research methodology in Africa. They suggested that there are three main factors which must be taken into consideration when doing research in African communities. First, one must be aware of the prevailing culture. (What types of activities are valued by the group?) Second, an assessment should be made of the intellectual capacities developed by the culture. The impoverishment of intellectual stimulation in the environment during early childhood may mean the child does not have the necessary foundations for learning when he enters school. In other words, what is the educational and cultural foundation of the society? Third, one must consider the psychometric or methodological difficulties presented, which are unique in each cultural setting (p. 256).

When talking about methodology it is necessary to say something further about Biesheuvel, who has been referred to as a "pioneer in the field of intercultural psychology" (Faverge & Flamagne, 1962). A glance at the bibliography at the end of this chapter will provide some indication of the extensive work he has done.

Biesheuvel's *The Study of African Ability* (1952b, c, d) was an attempt to assess what was known about the African as the result of previous research. He also raised questions about the validity of the studies and the research methodology employed. Biesheuvel acknowledged that there may be physiological differences between races, and that environment influences development, both quantitatively and qualitatively. However, he felt it had not been shown whether these differences vanished when environment was held constant. The only scientifically valid viewpoint to then was that African abilities were different from those of Westerners, and that cultural circumstances were a contributing factor. "It is not known from what genetic origins the mental abilities of Africans have developed nor how this relates to that of the Europeans under a controlled environment" (1952b, p. 11). Biesheuvel concluded that the next step was to develop different experimental and control techniques to provide a better picture of the African.

Biesheuvel also wrote extensive papers on the methodology involved in studying the attitudes of Africans (1958a, b). In these works he discussed the various methods available for studying attitudes, and he established three criteria to be met in designing tests for use in Africa: (1) the objectives should be appropriately matched with the test; (2) the assumptions implicit in the information of the research should be sound and consistent with what is known about the culture to be tested; and (3) the techniques used to obtain data must be effective. Biesheuvel felt that the main emphasis of psychological research should be on the "measurement of limits of modifiability of African behavior and towards a definition of the environmental factors which determine these limits" (1958b, p. 167).

In "Towards a Rationale for Testing Attainments and Abilities in Africa," Irvine (1966b) reviewed the research done in the area of cognitive measurement. This he followed with a discussion of the meaning of test scores in Africa and an elaboration on the problems involved in construction of tests in a non-Western society. Among these were that the test constructor should be aware of the lack of environmental supports to learning outside the school and cognizant of the standard of education provided by the local school. Currently there is a wide diversity in school quality. Irvine suggests that the effect of an individual school on test performance will decrease as a more uniform standard is achieved in terms of trained teachers and curriculum materials.

SUMMARY

To summarize the research done on intelligence and to give a picture of the current thinking on intelligence testing in Africa, references will be made to the works of three authors: Arthur Crijns, Oscar Ferron, and Irvine.

Both Crijns (1962) and Ferron (1964) surveyed the literature on testing with Africans and stated that it cannot be denied that Africans score lower than Westerners on tests which have been devised in Western cultures. Crijns continued by stating that, from the research available, a socio-cultural or environmental interpretation for this inferiority is the most plausible (p. 299). Ferron discussed environmental effects in more specific terms. He stated that the nature of the early environmental stimulation on the child appears to be one of the most important factors in later intellectual growth (p. v.).

It is important to note that both authors qualified their statements on the effects of environment. Crijns emphasized that environment may be important in determining test results, but that researchers must control for the significant environmental factors before completely discounting the nativistic viewpoint. Ferron felt that "environment" needed to be specifically defined if it was to explain differences in development. In assessing the effect of environment on intellectual growth, one must first ask what should be present in the environment to meet the requirements of optimal stimulation during the process of development.

In terms of the usefulness of Western tests in African societies, Crijns took the position that Western tests are not applicable in Africa because they are alien in cultural content and probe abilities valued in Western cultures which may not be operative in African intellectual behavior. This position was also taken by Irvine (1966b) who warned against judging the skills of people by using tests developed outside their culture.

In a discussion of the applicability of tests developed in African cultures, Irvine suggested: "Within Africa itself, as far as educational skills are concerned, the constructs [developed] can be applied across *African* cultures" (1966a, p. 6). He attempted to support this theory by suggesting that although African tribes present widely diverse culture patterns, the existing educational structures are based on Western education. Since the environment outside the school does not support the educational skills learned, the school becomes the only environment directly relevant to what is learned.

Irvine summarizes the feelings of many in his statement that unless psychologists in Africa can assess the motivational and social effects of a society on individual differences, research done on "African" intelligence will continue to be guided by the notion that intelligence is the same concept for every society.

BIBLIOGRAPHY

Abiola, E. T. "The Nature of Intellectual Development in Nigerian Children." *Teacher Education*, 1965, 6(1), pp. 37-58.

————. *The Intelligent Behavior of Nigerian Children.* Ibadan: African Education Press, 1966.

Anastasi, Anne, and Foley, John. *Differential Psychology: Individual and Group Differences in Behavior.* New York: Macmillan, 1949.

Andor, L. E. *Aptitudes and Abilities of the Black Man in Sub-Saharan Africa, 1784-1963: An Annotated Bibliography.* Johannesburg: National Institute for Personnel Research. South African Council for Scientific and Industrial Research, 1966.

Biesheuvel, Simon. *African Intelligence.* Johannesburg: Institute of Race Relations, 1943.

————. "Psychological Tests and Their Application to Non-European People." *The Yearbook of Education*, 1949, pp. 87-117.

————. "The Nation's Intelligence and Its Measurement." *South African Journal of Science*, 1952a, *49* (3-4), pp. 120-138.

————. "The Study of African Ability." *African Studies*, 1952b, *11*(1), pp. 1-14.

————. "The Study of African Ability, Part I. Intellectual Potentialities of Africans." *African Studies*, 1952c, *11*, pp. 45-57.

————. "The Study of African Ability, Part II. A Study of Some Research Problems." *African Studies*, 1952d, *11*, pp. 105-117.

————. "A Technique for Measuring Attitudes of Educated Africans." *South African Psychological Journal*, 1953, *4*.

————. "The Measurement of African Attitudes toward European Ethical Concepts, Customs, Laws, and Administration of Justice." *Journal of the National Institute of Personnel Research*, 1955, *6*, pp. 5-17.

————. "Objectives and Methods of African Psychological Research." *Journal of Social Psychology*, 1958a, *47*, pp. 161-168.

————. "Methodology in the Study of Attitudes of Africans." *Journal of Social Psychology*, 1958b, *47*, pp. 169-184.

————. "Report of the CSA Meeting of Specialists on the Basic Psychological Structures of African and Madagascan Populations; Commission for Technical Cooperation in Africa South of the Sahara." *Scientific Council for Africa South of the Sahara*, Publication No. 51, 1959.

————. "Detection and Fostering of Ability among Under-Developed Peoples." *Yearbook of Education*, 1962, pp. 337-352.

————, and Liddicoat, Renée. "The Effects of Cultural Factors on Intelligence Test Performance." *Journal of the National Institute of Personnel Research,* 1959, *8,* pp. 3-14.

Bradley, D. J. "The Ability of Black Groups to Produce Recognizable Patterns on the 7-Squares Test." *Journal of the National Institute of Personnel Research,* 1960, *8,* pp. 142-144.

Brimble, Arthur R. *The Construction of a Non-Verbal Test of Intelligence for Use in Northern Rhodesia in Selection for Education Or Training.* Unpublished masters thesis, London University, 1960-1961.

————. "The Construction of Non-Verbal Intelligence Test in Northern Rhodesia." *Rhodes-Livingstone Journal,* 1964, *34,* pp. 23-35.

Clarke, J. D. Performance Tests of Intelligence for Africa." *Overseas Education,* 1948, *20*(1), pp. 777-787; 1949, *20*(2), pp. 822-826.

Couch, Margaret. "A Select List of Intelligence and Other Tests Used With Non-Western Peoples." *Education Library Bulletin,* 1963, *18,* pp. 21-29.

Crijns, Arthur. "African Intelligence: A Critical Survey of Cross-Cultural Intelligence Research in Africa South of the Sahara." *Journal of Psychology,* 1962, *57,* pp. 283-301.

Dent, G. R. "An Investigation of Certain Aspects of Bantu Intelligence." *Department of Education, Arts and Science,* Pretoria: National Bureau of Education and Social Research, 1949.

Dewaay, G., and Dehondt, J. *Essai d'Adaptation du Test Buysée-Decroly (B-D) aux Enfants Congolais.* Léopoldville: Centre-Pilote D'Orientation Professionelle, 1958.

Dogbeh, Richard. "Intelligence and Education." *Présence Africaine,* English ed., 1961, *8*(37).

Doob, Leonard. "The Use of Different Test Items in Non-Literate Societies." *Public Opinion Quarterly,* 1957-58, *21,* pp. 499-504.

East African Aptitude Testing Unit. *A Presentation of the Results Obtained from Three Test Batteries Administered to a Group of African Secondary School Students in East Africa.* Nairobi, Kenya, 1965.

El-Abd, Hamed. *Three Facets of Mental Ability.* Makerere University College: Department of Educational Psychology, 1966.

Endemann, T. M. H. *Die Intelligensie van die Naturel in die Lig van Pedagogiese Bevindings aan die Bothsabelo Opleidingskook vir Naturelle.* Unpublished masters thesis, Pretoria, 1927.

Faverge, J. M., and Falmagne, J. C. "On the Interpretation of Data on Inter-Cultural Psychology." *Psychologica Africana,* 1962, *9,* pp. 22-36.

Ferron, Oscar. *A Study of Certain Factors Affecting the Tested Intelligence of Some Groups of West African Children.* Unpublished doctoral dissertation, London University, 1964.

————. "The Test Performance of 'Coloured' Children." *Educational Research,* 1965, *8,* pp. 42-57.

Fick, M. Lawrence. "Intelligence Test Results of Poor White, Native (Zulu), Coloured and Indian Children and the Educational and Social Implications." *South African Journal of Science,* 1929, *26,* pp. 904-920.

24

―――――. *Educability of Native Children of the Transvaal Compared with Other Groups on the Basis of Intelligence Tests.* Paper presented at the Education Fellowship Conference, July, 1934.

―――――. *An Individual Scale of General Intelligence for South Africa.* Pretoria: South African Council for Educational and Social Research, Research Series No. 7, 1939a.

―――――. *The Educability of the South African Native.* Pretoria: South African Council for Educational and Social Research, Research Series No. 8, 1939b.

Fontaine, Claude. "L'Utilisation Pratique des Méthodes de la Psychotechnique dans les Pays en Développement." *Bulletin du Secrétariat. D'État à la Santé Publique et aux Affaires Sociales,* 1961.

Fridjhon, Simone. "The PACTO Test, Symmetry and Intelligence." *Journal of the National Institute of Personnel Research,* 1961, *8,* pp. 180-188.

Ghilain, Jean. "Note sur le Testing de l'Éducabilité dans un Groupe de Noires Congolais." *Bulletin de l'Académie Royale des Sciences d'Outre-Mer,* Nouvelle Série, 1960, *6*(2).

Hudson, W., Lake, R. M., and Mbau, G. G. "A Study into the Applicability of a Counting Test Designed to Obtain Work Curves for Illiterate Africans." *Journal of the National Institute of Personnel Research,* 1957, *7,* pp. 71-74.

―――――, Mokoatle, B., and Mbau, G. G. "The Influence of Training and Practice on the Test and Work Performance of a Sample of African Workers." *Journal of the National Institute of Personnel Research,* 1958, *7,* pp. 88-94.

Irvine, Sidney. *Some Selection Problems at Post-Primary Level in Basutoland.* Department of Education. University College of Rhodesia and Nyasaland, 1962.

―――――. *Mental Abilities Survey.* Progress Report No. 4. University College of Rhodesia and Nyasaland, 1962-1964.

―――――. "Ability Testing in English-Speaking Africa: An Overview of Predictive and Comparative Studies." *Rhodes-Livingstone Journal,* 1963a, *34,* pp. 44-55.

―――――. *Some Practical and Theoretical Problems of General Ability Testing at the African Standard Six Level in Southern Rhodesia.* East African Institute of Social Research Paper, 1963b.

―――――. *A Psychological Study of Selection Problems at the End of Primary Schooling in Southern Rhodesia.* Unpublished doctoral dissertation, University of London, 1964.

―――――. "Adapting Tests to the Cultural Setting: A Comment." *Occupational Psychology,* 1965a, *39,* pp. 13-23.

―――――. *Selection for Secondary Education in Southern Rhodesia.* Faculty of Education Paper No. 4, University College, Salisbury, 1965b.

―――――. *The Factor Analysis of African Abilities and Attainments.* Paper presented to the 18th International Congress of Psychology: Moscow, August 4-11, 1966a.

―――――. "Towards a Rationale for Testing Attainments and Abilities in Africa." *British Journal of Educational Psychology,* 1966b, *36,* pp. 24-32.

Jahoda, Gustav. "Assessment of Abstract Behavior in a Non-Western Culture." *Journal of Abnormal and Social Psychology,* 1956, *53,* pp. 237-243.

King, V. *A Study of Individual Differences among Primary School Children in Sierra Leone with Specific Reference to the Selection of Those Children for Secondary Education.* Unpublished doctoral dissertation, London University, 1957.

LaRoche, J. L. "L'Analyse des Erreurs sur le Matrix 38." *Bulletin du Centre d'Études et Recherches Psychotechniques,* 1956, *6*(2).

Leblanc, Marie. "Adaptation Africaine et Comparison Interculturelle d'une Épreuve Projective: Test de Rosenzweig." *Revue de Psychologie Appliquée,* 1956, *6*(2), pp. 91-109.

Liddicoat, Renée, and Roberts, A. O. H. "Interim Standardization of the South African Version of the Wechsler-Bellevue Adult Intelligence Test." *Psychologica Africana,* 1962, *9,* pp. 273-285.

Loades, H. R., and Rich, S. G. "Binet Tests on South African Natives – Zulus." *Journal of Genetic Psychology,* 1917, *24,* pp. 373-383.

Loram, C. T. *The Education of the South African Native.* London: Longman's Green and Co., 1917.

MacArthur, R. S., Irvine, Sidney H., and Brimble, Arthur R. *The Northern Rhodesian Mental Ability Survey, 1963.* Lusaka: Rhodes-Livingstone Institute, 1964.

Maistriaux, Robert. "L'Intelligence Noire et Son Destin." *Problèmes d'Afrique Centrale (Bruxelles),* 1955, *30,* pp. 255-285; 1956, *31,* pp. 3-29.

―――――. "La Sous-Évolution des Noirs d'Afrique: Sa Nature, Ses Causes, Ses Remèdes." *Revue de Psychologie des Peuples,* 1956, *10*(1), pp. 167-189; (2), pp. 397-456.

McFie, John. "African Performance on an Intelligence Test." *Uganda Journal,* 1954, *18,* pp. 33-43.

―――――. "The Effect of Education on African Performance on a Group of Intellectual Tests." *British Journal of Educational Psychology,* 1961, *31,* pp. 232-240.

Morgan, P. "Observations and Findings on the 7-Square Test with Literate and Illiterate Black Groups in South Africa." *Journal of the National Institute of Personnel Research,* 1959, *8,* pp. 44-47.

Nadel, S. F. "The Application of Intelligence Tests in the Anthropological Field," in F. C. Bartlet, et al. (ed.). *The Study of Society: Methods and Problems.* London: Kegan Paul, 1939, pp. 190ff.

Nel, F. B. *Die Fantasie van Blanke en Naturelle Skoolgaande Kinders.* Amsterdam: Swets & Zeitlinger, 1935.

Nissen, H. W., Machover, S., and Kinder, Elaine. "A Study of Performance Tests Given to a Group of Native African Negro Children." *British Journal of Psychology,* 1935, *25,* pp. 308-355.

Notcutt, Bernard. "The Distribution of Scores on Raven's Progressive Matrix Test." *British Journal of Psychology,* 1949, *40*(2), pp. 68-71.

―――――. "The Measurement of Zulu Intelligence." *Journal of Social Research, Pretoria,* 1950, *1*(2), pp. 195-206.

Oliver, Richard. *General Intelligence Tests for Africans.* Nairobi: Government Printing Office, 1932a.

―――――. "The Musical Talent of Natives of East Africa." *British Journal of Psychology,* 1932b, *22,* pp. 333-343.

―――――. "The Comparison of Abilities of Races with Special Reference to East Africa." *East African Medical Journal,* 1932c, *9,* pp. 160-193.

―――――. "The Adaptation of Intelligence Tests to Tropical Africa." *Overseas Education,* 1933a, *4*(4), pp. 187-192; *5*(1), pp. 8-13.

————. *The Application of Psychological Tests to Certain Problems of Native Education in East Africa.* Unpublished doctoral dissertation, Edinburgh, 1933b.

————. "Mental Tests in the Study of the African." *Africa*, 1933c, 7(1), pp. 40-46.

————. "Comparison of Cultural Achievement." *Overseas Education*, 1934, 5, pp. 107-111.

Ombredane, André. "L'Exploration de la Mentalité des Noirs Congolais au Moyen d'une Épreuve Projective: Le Congo TAT." *Mémoires, Institut Royale Colonial Belge. Section des Sciences Morales et Politiques*, 1954, 37(5), pp. 1-243.

————. "Étude Psychologique des Noirs Asalampasu: I. Le Comportement Intellectuel dans l'Épreuve du Matrix-Couleur." *Mémoires, Académie Royale des Sciences Coloniales. Classe des Sciences Morales et Politiques*, 1956, 6(3).

————. "Étude Psychotechnique des Baluba: I. Application Expérimentale du Test d'Intelligence, Matrix 38 à 485 Noirs Baluba." *Mémoires, Académie Royale des Sciences Coloniales. Classe des Sciences Morales et Politiques*, 1957, 6(6).

————. "Primitive Intellectual Development." *Journal of Education*, 1957, 89, pp. 385-387.

————. "Etude Psychologique des Noirs Asalampasu: II. Analyse de Comportement dans le Test des Relations Spatiales de Minnesota." *Mémoires, Académie Royale des Sciences Coloniales, Classe des Sciences Morales et Politiques*, 1958, 6(7).

————, Bertelson, .Paul, and Beniest-Noirot, Elaine. "Speed and Accuracy of Performance of an African Native Population and of Belgian Children on a Paper and Pencil Perceptual Test." *Journal of Social Psychology*, 1958, 47, pp. 327-337.

————, and Robaye, F. "Le Problème de L'Expuration des Résultats des Tests d'Intelligence Étudié sur le Matrix-Couleur: Comparison des Techniques de Reduplication et d'Explication." *Bulletin du Centre d'Études et Recherches Psychotechniques*, 1953, 2, pp. 3-17.

Pillner, A. E. G. *Objective Testing in West Africa.* Report to the British Council, 1964.

Porteus, S. D. "Race and Social Differences in Performance Tests." *Genetic Psychology.* Monograph No. 8, 1930.

————. *Primitive Intelligence and Environment.* New York: Macmillan, 1937.

Price-Williams, Douglas R. "Analysis of an Intelligence Test Used in Rural Areas of Central Nigeria." *Overseas Education*, 1961, 33(3), pp. 124-133.

Raven, J. C. "The Comparative Assessment of Intellectual Ability." *British Journal of Psychology*, 1948, 39, pp. 12-19.

Rich, S. G. "Binet-Simon Tests on Zulus." *South African Journal of Science*, 1918, 14, pp. 477-482.

Ritchie, J. F. *The African Child as Suckling and as Adult (A Psychological Study).* Rhodes-Livingstone Institute, Paper No. 9, 1943.

Robaye, F., and Plumail, H. "Résultats d'une Application Répétée de Matrix-Couleur à une Population de Noirs Congolais." *Bulletin du Centre d'Études et Recherches Psychotechniques*, 1956, 6, pp. 129-147.

Rosseau, H. J. "Ability in a Multi-Cultural Community: Rhodesia and Nyasaland." *Yearbook of Education*, 1962, pp. 328-336.

Scott, G. C. "Measuring Sudanese Intelligence." *British Journal of Educational Psychology*, 1950, 20(1), pp. 43-54.

Silvey, Jonathan. *Ability Testing Results from Junior Secondary Schools in Buganda.* East African Institute of Social Research Conference Paper No. 166, 1963a.

———. *Preliminary Thoughts on Testing and Educational Selection in Africa.* East African Institute of Social Research Conference Paper No. 167, 1963b.

———. *Testing Ability Tests: Issues in the Measurement of Ability among African Schoolboys.* East African Institute of Social Research Conference Paper, 1963c.

———. "Aptitude Testing and Educational Selection in Africa." *Rhodes-Livingstone Journal,* 1964, *34*, pp. 9-22.

Somerset, H. C. A. *Success and Failure in School Certificate.* East African Institute of Social Research Conference Paper, 1966.

Swarz, P. A. *Aptitude Tests for Use in the Developing Nations.* Pittsburgh: American Institute for Research, 1961.

———. "Adapting Tests to the Cultural Setting." *Journal of Educational and Psychological Measurement,* 1963, *23*, pp. 673-686.

Taylor, Andrew. (ed.) *Educational and Occupational Selection in West Africa.* London: Oxford University Press, 1962.

VanRensburg, Jansen. *The Learning Ability of the South African Native Compared with That of the European.* Pretoria: South African Council for Educational and Sociological Research Series No. 5, 1938.

Verhaegen, Paul, and Laroche, J. L. "Some Methodological Considerations Concerning the Study of Aptitudes and the Elaboration of Psychological Tests for African Natives." *Journal of Social Psychology,* 1958, *47*, pp. 249-256.

Vernon, P. E. "Race and Intelligence." *Eugenics Review,* 1959, *60*, pp. 99-101.

———. *Intelligence and Intelligence Tests.* London: University of London Press, 1960.

———. *The Structure of Human Abilities.* London: Methuen, 1961.

———. *Cross-Cultural Studies of Abilities.* National Institute of Education, Makerere University College, Kampala, Uganda, 1966.

———. *Abilities and Educational Attainments in an East African Environment.* National Institute of Education, Makerere University College, Kampala, Uganda, 1967.

Wilrocks, R. W. *The South African Group Test of Intelligence: Description and Directions.* Pro-Ecclesis-Drukkery, (no date).

———. "The Growth and Distribution of Intelligence." *Journal of Genetic Psychology,* 1932, *6*.

Winterbottom, J. M. "Can We Measure the African's Intelligence?" *Rhodes-Livingstone Journal,* 1948, *6*, pp. 53-63.

Wintringer, G. "Considérations sur l'Intelligence du Noir Africain." *Revue de Psychologie des Peuples,* 1955, *10*, pp. 37-55.

III. Physiological Development

Old peoples' walking teaches young ones to walk.
Kikuyu Proverb

In that large section of the population which is without obvious physical symptoms of nutritional disease and yet is undernourished, the impairment of efficiency is often likely to be predominantly mental. . . . The psychological changes induced by under-nutrition, though more difficult to measure, seem to be just as typical as are the physical changes.
Carothers, 1953, p. 41.

While various authors were looking into the philosophical and psychological differences between races, studies were also being done on the physiological aspects of growth. It is generally recognized that there are physical differences between races, yet there has been no conclusive research into the relationship between these differences and intellectual functioning. Since the main emphasis of this chapter and bibliography is on cognitive development, only those studies of physiological development which may have implications for cognitive growth are included.

Extensive work on the physiological development of young children has been done by Marcelle Geber and R. F. A. Dean in East Africa, mainly among the Baganda. While studying the effects of kwashiorkor on infants, Geber also collected data on the normal growth pattern of African children. During this time she became aware of the fact that African infants were better developed physically than their European counterparts. Her description of the African child is paraphrased:

> On the first day the African child is able to hold his head while in a sitting position and is able to focus his gaze. At four months he sits without support and can lean forward and regain his balance. He stands upright on his own at eight months and is able to walk at ten months. At eleven months the child can pick up a small object using his thumb and index finger. At fourteen months he can run (Geber, 1962, p. 54).

Geber found that the African child not only exhibits rapid physical development, but is also able to communicate with others at a younger age. He seems to have greater ability to adapt himself to the objects around him

29

and use them quicker. At the age of six months the African child is two or three months ahead of his European counterpart.

To study the physical development of the African child, Geber used a series of Gesell tests on children, from birth to more than three years of age. The trend shown in her statistics indicates that the younger the African child is, the more advanced he is over his European counterpart. By the age of three the performance of the European child is the same as that of the African. These same results were found by Solange Falade (1955), who observed 180 children in Dakar, and by Vouilloux (1959) in the Cameroons. Geber's sample included 308 children, 51 of which were tested a second time a year later. Some of her children were tested as many as five times at yearly intervals (Geber, 1958b).

After noting the early precocity of African children, Geber began to ask why this declined as the child grew. By examining the data, she discovered that after weaning the children showed a marked difference in behavior and in test results. This she attributed to the effects of weaning which appear to be accompanied by a change in the mother's attitude toward the child. After weaning the child is given less attention and the mother is no longer available constantly, nor is she as indulgent or accepting of the child (1957, p. 1063). It is interesting to note that African children reared in the same pattern as their European counterparts follow the developmental pattern of Western growth rather than that of the traditionally-reared African (ibid.). Geber was also interested in looking into the factors which contribute to the African's precocity, and how this precocity could be maintained. She also raised the question of whether this physical precocity has an intellectual counterpart.*

M. Vincent (1954) observed the physical development of children in Ruanda-Urundi. He concluded that their late pubertal development is due to the social and nutritional elements of the culture. Vincent's article also contains a discussion of the environmental factors influencing the physical and psychological development of the child.

Some of the cultural factors that may affect the child's growth are described by Dean (1962), who has done extensive work in Uganda. Dean found that the frequency of nutritional diseases in Uganda has led Baganda parents to conclude that these diseases are part of the child's normal development, for when a child is born the older is weaned and his diet becomes poorer. Research by Hebe Welbourn (1963) showed that at the same time the child loses the emotional support his mother provided. This may also lead to a loss of appetite which adds to the malnutrition.

---

*For a review of the studies by Geber, and those of Falade, as well as others related to the physical development of Africans, see Biesheuvel, 1959, 1963.

KWASHIORKOR: PHYSIOLOGICAL AND PSYCHOLOGICAL EFFECTS

One fairly common disease throughout Africa which results from malnutrition is kwashiorkor. The malnutrition is specifically defined as a deficiency of protein in the diet during the child's second or third year. Although kwashiorkor may be strictly physiological, there seems to be an increasing body of knowledge to suggest that this disease also has a notable psychological component.

In a laboratory setting, where the environment was controlled, J. J. Cowley and R. D. Griesel did some experiments with white rats to look at the possible effects of kwashiorkor on physical and mental development. The results indicated that pups of rats given a low protein diet were lower in I.Q. and more emotional than the pups of parents given a normal diet. There was no effect on the adult (1959). In the second generation there was evidence of a general retardation of growth. The authors found that retardation in development is evident at an early age and, that where there is a critical period for establishing certain response patterns, retardation of development may lead to permanent mental disability later in life (1963). Cowley and Griesel were not ready to commit themselves to the position that similar characteristics would be found in children suffering from kwashiorkor, but they felt that research should be done to see if kwashiorkor affected critical learning periods in children.

The works of Trowell, Davies, and Dean (1952, 1954) indicated that in cases where protein deficiency is serious there exists a particular psychological system. In both children and adults this is characterized by "mental apathy" and "slowness and feebleness of movement" (1954, pp. 100-101). Two aspects of this psychological system which have particular relevance to the cognitive growth of the child are that he loses all "normal curiosity and desire for exploration that is natural to the child." and "seems to show no interest in his surroundings" (1954, p. 256).

An extensive study of the effects of kwashiorkor on psychological and physiological functioning was undertaken by Geber and Dean (1956). They studied 25 children who, when admitted to the hospital, were diagnosed as having kwashiorkor. The children ranged in age from one to three. On admission they were generally inert and uninterested in their environment, cried continuously, refused to eat, and presented a picture of misery. Extensive histories were done on each child's background, and observations were made throughout his stay in the hospital – particularly of the relationship between the child and his mother. Gesell tests were then administered to the children. A full discussion of tests used and the results obtained are included in the Geber and Dean article.

From their work, Geber and Dean concluded that there is a definite psychological component to kwashiorkor that accompanies no other disease.

The investigators also concluded that a child's "mental structure" determines to a large extent the occurrence and severity of kwashiorkor. A child who has developed a good relationship with his mother is not as emotionally threatened by weaning as the child who is unsure of his mother even before weaning, and is thus not as susceptible to kwashiorkor. The authors expressed the hope that longitudinal studies will be undertaken to assess the long range effects of kwashiorkor on physical and psychological development.

Other investigators whose works indicated that there was a psychological component to kwashiorkor include: Williams (1938), Purcell (1939), and Russell (1946) who worked in West Africa; Gelfand (1946) in Kenya; and Doucet (1946) in the Belgian Congo. One study that indicated that there were no developmental differences between Africans who had and had not suffered malnutrition was reported by Akim, McFie, and Sebigajju (1956).

Generally speaking, the above authors referred to cases of extreme deficiency. To what extent might it be expected that some of these same behavioral symptoms exist in less severe cases of deficiency? Leonard Doob (1961) hypothesized that a culture that taboos the drinking of milk and offers no other protein substitute will exhibit some diminished form of the same psychological characteristics described above (p. 226).

Others who have studied and written extensively on child health and its possible effects on physical and mental development include Welbourn, D. B. Jeliffe, F. J. Bennett and J. Lutwama in Uganda. In order to understand the effects of the cultural practices on health, these individuals have done extensive work on child-rearing practices in Buganda. Since diseases have physical and psychological components, they feel that in order to treat a disease it is important to understand the cultural milieu surrounding the child. Their work has implications for those interested specifically in the effects of diseases such as kwashiorkor on the mental development of the child in Africa.

BIBLIOGRAPHY

Akim, B., McFie, John, and Sebigajju, E. *Journal of Tropical Pediatrics,* 1956, 2, pp. 159-165.

Biesheuvel, Simon. "Report of the CSA Meeting of Specialists on the Basic Psychological Structure of African and Madagascan Populations; Commission for Technical Cooperation in Africa South of the Sahara." *Scientific Council for Africa South of the Sahara.* Publication No. 51, 1959.

Bennett, F. J., and Lutwama, J. S. W. *Health: A Challenge to African Schools.* London: Longman's Green & UNICEF, 1967.

Brock, J. F., and Autret, M. *Kwashiorkor in Africa.* W.H.O. Monograph Series 8, 1952.

Burgess, H. J. L., and Burgess, A. P. "The Growth of Some Uganda Schoolgirls." *East African Medical Journal,* 1965, 42, pp. 135-142.

Carothers, J. C. *The African Mind in Health and Disease.* Geneva: W.H.O., 1953.

Clark, M. "Kwashiorkor." *East African Medical Journal,* 1951, *28,* p. 229.

Cowley, J. J., and Griesel, R. D. "Some Effects of a Low Protein Diet on a First Filial Generation of White Rats." *Journal of Genetic Psychology,* 1959, *95,* pp. 187-201.

————. "The Development of Second Generation Low Protein Rats." *Journal of Genetic Psychology,* 1963, *103,* pp. 233-242.

Crijns, Arthur. "African Intelligence: A Critical Survey of Cross-Cultural Research in Africa South of the Sahara." *Journal of Social Psychology,* 1962, 57, pp. 283-301.

Dean, R. F. A. "Standards for African Children and the Influence of Nutrition." *Journal of Tropical and Medical Hygiene,* 1954, *57,* pp. 283-289.

————. "Health Education and Protein-Calorie Malnutrition." *Journal of Tropical Medicine,* 1962.

Doob, Leonard. *Communication in Africa: A Search for Boundaries.* New Haven: Yale University Press, 1961.

Doucet, G. "Le 'Mbuaki' ou Maladie de Carence Observée au Kwango." *Revue des Sciences Médicale en Congo Belge.* 1946, *5,* pp. 261 ff.

Falade, Solange. *Le Développement Psycho-Moteur du Jeune Africain Originaire de Sénégal au Cours de Sa Première Anneé.* Paris: Foulon, 1955.

Geber, Marcelle "Développement Psycho-Moteur de l'Enfant Africain," *Courrier,* 1955, *6,* pp. 17-28.

————. "L'Enfant Africain Occidentalisé et de Niveau Social Supérieur en Ouganda." *Courrier,* 1958a, *8,* pp. 517-523.

————. "The Psychomotor Development of African Children in the First Year and the Influence of Maternal Behavior." *Journal of Social Psychology,* 1958b, *47,* pp. 185-195.

————. "Problèmes Posés par le Développement du Jeune Enfant Africain en Fonction de Son Milieu Social, 1960." *Le Travail Humain,* 1960, *23,* pp. 97-111.

————. "Longitudinal Study and Psychomotor Development among Baganda Children. Proceedings of the XIV International Congress of Applied Psychology." *Child and Education.* Copenhagen, 1962.

————, and Dean, R. F. A. "Psychological Factors in the Etiology of Kwashiorkor." *Bulletin, W.H.O.,* 1955, *12*(3), pp. 471-475.

————. "The Psychological Changes Accompanying Kwashiorkor." *Courrier,* 1956, *6*(1), pp. 3-15.

————. "Gesell Tests on African Children." *Pediatrics,* 1957a, *20,* pp. 1055-1065.

————. "The State of Development of Newborn African Children." *Lancet,* 1957b, *272,* pp. 1216-1219.

————. "Psychomotor Development in African Children: The Effects of Social Class and the Need for Improved Tests." *Bulletin, W.H.O.,* 1958, *18,* pp. 471-476.

Gelfand, M. "Kwashiorkor," *Clinical Procedures,* 1946, *5,* p. 135.

"Health Education and the Mother and Child in East Africa." *Journal of Tropical Medicine and Hygiene,* 1962.

Jelliffe, D. B. "Cultural Variation and the Practical Pediatrician." *Journal of Pediatrics,* 1956, *49.*

————, and Bennett, F. J. "Indigenous Medical Systems and Child Health." *Journal of Pediatrics,* 1960, *57,* pp. 248-261.

34

————. "Cultural and Anthropological Factors in Infant and Maternal Nutrition." *Federal Proceedings,* 1961, *20.*

————, *et al.* "Custom and Child Health in Buganda." *Tropical and Geographical Medicine,* 1963, *15,* pp. 121-157.

Mundy-Castle, A. C., McKiever, B. L., and Prinsloo, T. "A Comparative Study of the Electroencephalograms of Normal Africans and Europeans of Southern Africa." *EEG Clinic of Neurophysiology,* 1953, *5,* pp. 533-543.

————, and Nelson, G. K. "Intelligence, Personality and Brain Rhythms in a Socially Isolated Community." *Nature,* 1960, *185,* pp. 484-485.

————. "A Neuropsychological Study of the Knysna Forest Workers." *Psychologica Africana,* 1962, *9,* pp. 240-272.

Nelson, G. K., and Dean, R. F. A. "The Electroencephalogram in African Children: Effects of Kwashiorkor and a Note on the Newborn." *Bulletin: W.H.O.,* 1959, *21,* pp. 779-782.

Purcell, F. M. *Diet and Ill-Health in the Forest Country of the Gold Coast.* London: H. K. Lewis and Co., 1939.

Russell, B. A. S. "Malnutrition in Children Under Three Years of Age in Ashanti, West Africa." *Archives of Disease in Childhood,* 1946, *21,* p. 110ff.

Trowell, H. C., Davies, J. N. P., and Dean, R. F. A. "Kwashiorkor. II. Clinical Picture, Pathology and Differential Diagnosis." *British Medical Journal,* 1952, *2,* p. 798ff.

————. *Kwashiorkor.* London: Edward Arnold Ltd., 1954.

Vincent, M. "L'Enfant au Ruanda-Urundi." *Mémoires de la Section des Sciences Naturelles et Médicales de l'Institut Royal Belge,* 1954, *23,* p. 6ff.

Vouilloux, "Étude de la Psycho-Motricité d'Enfants Africains au Caméroun: Tests de Gesell et Réflexes Archaiques." *Journal de la Société des Africanistes,* 1959, *29*(1), pp. 11-18.

Welbourn, Hebe. *The Coronation Book of Child Health in Buganda.* Kampala: Uganda Bookshop, 1953.

————. "Health Education for the Younger Child. *Journal of Tropical Medicine and Hygiene,* 1962.

————. "Custom and Child Health in Buganda: 2. Methods of Child Rearing." *Journal of Tropical and Geographical Medicine,* 1963, *15,* pp. 124-133.

Williams, C. D. "Child Health in the Gold Coast." *Lancet,* 1938, *1,* p. 97ff.

IV. Socialization

Culture can produce and maintain profound differences even in those reactions which psychologists have regarded as basic to all behavior. To describe a race or a people as innately aggressive or peaceable, sedentary or nomadic, promiscuous or puritanical, overlooks the fact that culture may be entirely responsible.

Otto Klineberg, 1935, pp. 273-274.

One might say that the average [African] has an understanding of the European culture comparable to that of the European child. But, conversely, one could state that the average White has an understanding of the African world which resembles that of an African child.

Ombredane, 1954, p. 41.

This chapter deals with aspects of the socialization process which may affect the mental growth and development of the child. The first part includes references on child-rearing practices, the second discusses aspects of traditional and modern education. Part three deals with what various authors consider to be the effects of socialization on the personality development of the individual, part four with descriptions and studies of the acculturation level of various African peoples.

CHILD-REARING PRACTICES

Don't take the boy's [hoe] from him [and do his work] for he will throw it down when he finds it too hot to work.

Hausa Proverb

The work done by anthropologists has yielded detailed ethnographic sketches of many cultures in Africa. These sketches generally include a description of child-rearing practices, since they are an integral part of the socialization process. The ethnographic material included in this review either focuses on childhood in a specific tribe or contains hypotheses about the effects of child-rearing practices on the cognitive growth of the child.

A historical look at anthropology indicates that as early as 1906 interest was shown in the African child. In that year there appeared a book by Dudley

35

Kidd called *Savage Childhood: A Study of Kafir Children.** Kidd was aware of the importance of studying the child in order to better understand the society. His book, very thorough in its coverage of the phases of childhood and the activities of the African child, includes a discussion of the play of children and a section which contains traditional stories. It has many insights that can be quite valuable if one is able to read between the condescending tone and value judgments. Otto Raum (1940) described *Savage Childhood* as a book with a "touch of poetic truthfulness . . . which makes it valuable for all time" (p. 26).

Another book that looked specifically at children in Africa was N. Miller's *The Child in Primitive Society* (1928). It contains a summary of all anthropological works that included a description of the child in African society. The picture of childhood in a tribal situation as compiled by Miller is not enviable, the child's life being "grim and earnest among . . . folk of a simple culture" (p. 121). Traditional education, Miller noted, is mainly through imitation and is basically self-acquired. Parents and elders only occasionally intervene "to induce the desirable physical and mental attributes that make for efficiency" (p. 180). The climax of the child's education comes when he or she is initiated and thus becomes an adult in the society. Miller felt that traditional education was binding and limiting to the individual's expression of himself, and that primitive societies were characterized by a "groping need for compelling conformity" (p. 252). Miller's tendency to make generalizations leads to some inconsistencies in his statements and causes him to overlook the immense diversity among African cultures. However, the book is comprehensive and useful as a reference work on early anthropological recordings in Africa.

J. F. Ritchie (1943, 1944), who was interested in the personality development of the African, looked at child-rearing practices in Rhodesia, and reached the conclusion that the African personality is unstable and somewhat arrested in mental development (1944, p. 55). This, he said, is due to the nature of early infant life, which he describes as follows:

> Because of the indulgent first year, the child gains a feeling of omnipotence. After weaning he is overwhelmed by feelings of hostility and impotence because he can no longer have the attention and nurturance of the first year. The world is thus divided into two forces: a benevolent power which would give him everything for nothing (the mother, during his first year), and a malevolent force which would deprive him even of life itself (again, the mother, due to the severe weaning). This high contrast in feelings of acceptance makes him

*Kafir is the term used by Europeans to describe all black people in Africa irrespective of their race and origin, and has come to be used as an insult among Africans themselves.

dependent on a mother or mother-surrogate all his life. The individual personality is never liberated and brought under conscious rational control and self realization is thus unknown. . . . (1943, p. 61).

According to Ritchie, these personality characteristics can be found in all aspects of the African's life, from his schooling to his adult life. Later authors have been critical of Ritchie's work, because his theory of African emotional adjustment and consequent intellectual impairment is not soundly supported, and his analysis of customs is totally in terms of Western ideas and values (Marwick, 1949).

J. C. Carothers (1953, 1954) picked up Ritchie's theme and developed it even further. Carothers began *The African Mind in Health and Disease* with a discussion of the physical background of the African. This included a discussion of race followed by a description of the African continent, which was pictured as a harsh, extremely difficult place to live. Aspects of the African's environment were also discussed, such as types of physical diseases and some of their effects on growth and development. Carothers' description of climate, nutritional factors, and cultural characteristics are generalized to the whole of Africa, as are child-rearing practices, which he focused on in describing the development of the African personality.

Carothers, as Ritchie before him, placed great emphasis on the importance of weaning methods, which are characterized by a switch from a lengthy period of indulgence to a loss of attention and a feeling of alienation from the mother. After discussing various aspects of a child's life and education— which he saw as producing mental uniformity, a basically static community, and the development of a good rote memory — Carothers concluded that the African does not show "total personality integration in a situation which is not defined traditionally. The African tends to act impulsively with little or no reference to past experience, present perception, or future implications" (1953, p. 107).

Soon after Carothers' book appeared, Melville Herskovits (1954) wrote a review of it, criticizing Carothers on several points. First, although Carothers stated that he realized Africa presents many cultures, he continued to make generalizations about the total African culture. Second, Carothers did not make use of the current ethnographic material available. By using material available, he would not have over-simplified the variations in social behavior which exist in Africa. Third, Carothers did not consult authorities in relevant fields before the book was published in order to check on his data. Herskovits stated that Carothers does not treat the African as a second-class citizen, but as a second-rate performer on the cultural stage. The main theme of Carothers' monograph, stated Herskovits, was that:

African culture has developed on such lines as to reduce the exigencies of living to a minimum, and that the integration which the rural African apparently achieves is founded on the continuing support afforded by his culture and he has but little independent existence in himself (p. 110).

Margaret Read's book, *Children of Their Fathers* (1959), presents a picture of a child's life in the Ngoni tribe in Nyasaland, in which she describes the ideas the society perpetuates and how the child learns them. Among the most important qualities for which the children are trained are: (1) respect; (2) honor; (3) physical strength – closely associated with moral courage; (4) persistence and thoroughness in all tasks; (5) wisdom – contrasted with cleverness – which includes knowledge, good judgment, ability to control people and to keep at peace, and skill in using speech; and (6) dignity (p. 48).

Read noted several facets of Ngoni life which she felt were worth studying further, among them the amount of security offered to the child through his wide primary group, the actual pattern of inter-personal relationships and their possible effects, and a picture of the ideal personality within the culture. Among her discoveries, Read found that the child gains a feeling of security early because he is trained at a young age and knows what his society expects of him in all situations. As well as being descriptive of the Ngoni peoples, Read's book provides those interested in African children with many ideas worth exploring.

Another anlaysis of child-rearing practices, especially the relationship between the mother and the child, was done among the Ganda in Uganda by Mary Ainsworth (1967). Ainsworth did in-depth case studies of 28 children between the ages of one and fifteen months in order to study the development of attachment in children.

She concluded that environmental factors may have a significant effect on the development of the relations between the child and those in positions to influence him. She also found that genetic factors are not overwhelmingly important, that what appear to be more crucial are infant-care practices (p. 387). Ainsworth indicated that of the measures she was using to assess attachment, three were particularly important: the amount of care the mother gives the child; the degree of the mother's interest in and enjoyment of the child; and the maternal attitude toward breast feeding, in that those who enjoyed it developed better relations with their children.

One of the most extensive descriptions of an African childhood is provided by Robert and Barbara LeVine (1963), who summarized infancy "as the period between birth and weaning when the greatest amount of attention is paid to [the child's] needs and the least effort directed toward [the child's] training" (p. 137). At the end of infancy the child is a dependent individual who, while capable of making demands for food and protection of his mother and others who care for him, is quiet and timid in approaching the physical environment and new situations (p. 147). The LeVines noted that infancy ends when the child is weaned, often a quite severe process, since the mother feels that the quicker it is accomplished the easier it will be for her and the child. During weaning, when the child cries, the mother either ignores or punishes the child, and provides no emotional substitute for the breast. The child senses that emotionally his mother has abandoned him (p. 151).

Weaning is the first of a series of stages through which the child passes between the ages of eighteen months and ten years. Others include toilet training and responsibility training, and usually the birth of a sibling. During this period the child is severely punished for his infantile dependence behavior, and begins to learn new patterns of behavior which are part of the adult society. Responsibility for his training is the mother's, but due to the heavy demands of agriculture and the need to provide for the family, the mother is unable to spend much time with her children.

One of the primary aims of child training is to teach obedience. This obedience is often enforced through the use of corporal punishment, the severity of which depends on the mood of the parent. Another method of enforcement is through fear; children learn to be afraid of animals, darkness, spirits, and the unknown. A good child is an obedient child. As the authors have noted: "Obedience rather than enterprise or initiative is considered to be the key to success in the contemporary setting" (p. 181). This emphasis on obedience is the deciding influence on whether the child will be sent to school — the child who will not obey the teacher will not be sent. His intelligence is gauged by his respect and filial piety.

Barbara LeVine (1962) examined child-rearing practices among the Yoruba by having secondary school students write two essays on experiences they had as children. One was about a situation in which they received praise, the other of an instance in which they were punished. The essays were to include the age at which the event occurred, the act itself, and the method and agent of reward or punishment. In analyzing instances of praise, she found that academic achievement was rewarded most often. Verbal praise was the most frequent method, with material rewards of a utilitarian nature second. Parents provided more than 50 per cent of the rewards. She also found that parents of the same sex as the subject provided more rewards than parents of the opposite sex. Punishment was most often given when a child failed to obey a standing rule. Boys would deliberately do something they were told not to do, but girls were less openly defiant and would frequently do such things as steal food when they knew no one saw them. It is interesting to note that more punishments than rewards were given by parents, and that the most frequent means of punishment was physical. In their essays, the girls gave more emphasis to verbal behavior, while the boys recorded more physical aggression responses both in the acts and their consequences.

Renée Liddicoat and Constance Koza (1963), using an adaptation of Gesell's language test, looked at child-rearing practices in terms of their effect on language development. They noted that children in the care of older siblings developed language ability faster, for two reasons. First, they had to learn to stand on their own, and second, they had to assert themselves in order to be accepted by the older children who took care of them. Those children under the care of adults were more pampered, and there was less need for them to communicate their desires since these were often anticipated.

In looking at the intellectual growth of West African children, Oscar Ferron (1964) concluded that the existing child-rearing practices in West Africa were detrimental to the growth of Western skills (p. 60). Some of the practices Ferron saw as contributing to low test quotients include: a lack of appropriate verbal stimulation, the relative absence of an atmosphere of approval and encouragement, the lack of adult attention, the general illiteracy of the mother, a mechanical approach to learning, and a lack of encouragement to children to ask questions and explore their environment (pp. 435-437).

Barrington–Kaye (1962) produced what he termed an "impressionistic survey" of child-rearing practices in Ghana. His work, based on preliminary studies made by 37 students at the University College of Ghana, emphasized three considerations that should be made when evaluating the book: (1) individual variations in reporters, (2) the possibility that the data relates to the ideal rather than the normal behavior, and (3) the fact that valid inferences about the frequency of the behavior cannot be made (p. 9).

His book divides a child's life into its various phases. In each section there is an overview of Ghana in general, followed by a description of the specific practices in each tribal area. This approach leads to repetition and makes the book difficult to read. However, the book contains valuable material for those interested in social science research, and is a first attempt to analyze and hypothesize about the stages of social and moral development of children in Ghana.

While Barrington-Kaye used reports from students to write his book, the first collection of childhood experiences actually written by Africans was compiled and edited by Lorene Fox (1967). Her book contains the works of three authors from three different tribes in East Africa, who describe their childhood and the effects it had on their lives. Valuable contributions of this book are the authors' discussions of present day methods of child rearing which have evolved in their villages as a result of continually growing contact with a larger world.

Biesheuvel (1959b) provides a summary of the current state of knowledge and trend of thought about child-care practices throughout Africa: (1) *Birth and Pre-birth*. The child is highly desired in most African cultures, and this may decrease birth trauma. It is hypothesized that this partially accounts for African children's advanced state of physical development at birth (see Chapter 3). A favorable affective climate is considered most important and probably affects development of a psychological nature as well. (2) *Nursing period.* The child is given complete security from birth to weaning. Some psychologists feel that this, when followed by the trauma of weaning, hampers the development of a well-integrated personality. (3) *Weaning.* Weaning practices differ greatly throughout Africa, and this must be considered in discussions of the child's later development. The variety of weaning practices has led to varying opinions about their effects on the psychological development of the child.

Verhaegen (1959) summarizes the personality of the African in the Congo as follows: The child is indulged during the first year, and perhaps becomes fixed at this stage since it provided him with such satisfaction. Between the ages of two and six, he is effectively isolated from adults and has little opportunity to identify with an adult figure. This lack of identity leads to an absence of guilt. Verhaegen continues by discussing the fact that early childhood experiences establish the foundation of the personality, but concludes:

> We must not, however, fail to take into account the contributions and adjustments that are made once he starts to school, especially in Africa today where, from this time onwards, his contacts with values, ideas and persons belonging to a so-called universal culture, become increasingly operative (p. 9).

EDUCATION: TRADITIONAL AND MODERN

A man's disposition, or nature, precedes his education, and every one has his own.

Hausa Proverb

Two important parts of the socialization process are the formal and informal educational systems to which the child is exposed. This section begins with a discussion of traditional education and is followed by references to the current educational system and its relationship to African cultures. It concludes with a review of recent works which suggest ways in which traditional and Western culture can be synthesized to create an educational system relevant to the African child.

In the traditional society all aspects of education are an integral part of daily life. Fortes (1938) referred to traditional education as the "by-product of the cultural routine" (p. 1). His work, *Social and Psychological Aspects of Education in Taleland,* is a description of traditional education among the

Tallensi in West Africa. Fortes stated that in Tale society the reality orientation of the child is also that of the adult. Children take part in adult activities to the full extent of their age and ability. Education is a joint enterprise: the adults are eager to teach, the children eager to learn. Adults are tolerant of children's learning habits and do not push them beyond their readiness and capability. Fortes summarized the education of the Tale child as the "gradual acquisition of an ensemble of *interests, observances and skills*" (p. 22).

Raum's work, *Chagga Childhood* (1940), was aimed at "studying the native educational system in its widest sense in order to assess what place there is in that system for the 'alien' contribution of European schools" (p. vii). His study included a survey of works on education to that time, as well as those which dealt with the education of primitive children. He described the activities of the Chagga child and illustrated how education permeates all aspects of his life. In contrast, Western education is viewed by the Chagga people as artificial, transitory, and intermittent. In discussing the cognitive growth of Africans, Raum noted that "The mental growth in all races becomes increasingly defined and differentiated in its expression by the cultural medium. The African child's mental reactions may therefore be expected to adapt themselves to the culture-contact situation" (p. 395). Western education, he commented, has failed to take into consideration the "culture-contact" situation present in African tribes, and must learn to use the local environment more effectively.

F. Denis (1951), who worked in the Congo, was interested in the relationship between the educational system in traditional society and the psychological development of the African. He felt that an analysis of traditional education revealed that the African is satisfied with naive answers because his mind is able to grasp only relationships of direct dependence (p. 350).

Carothers (1953, 1954) found that the education of the African child is traditionally verbal, musical, dramatic, and emotional. The child exists in a world of sound, in contrast to the European who lives in a world of sight.

An understanding of the world we live in and the development of our objective attitudes and mature responsibility depend upon a well-developed sense of spatial and temporal causal relationships and these in turn depend on habits of visual as opposed to auditory synthesis (1953, p. 103).

Assuming that this pattern of learning is valid, Carothers concluded that Western education is irrelevant in many ways for the African, for he has no experience on which to build school knowledge.

Welbourn (1962, 1963) was interested in traditional education as it relates to the health of the Baganda child, and described both the traditional patterns of child rearing and patterns found in urban societies in Uganda today (1963). Part of this work included remarks on the effects of formal schooling on the child. Often, going to school helps the child to

> escape from the drudgery and restrictions at home and move into a freer atmosphere at school. Unfortunately very few children stay at school for very long. They return home dissatisfied with a feeling that authority has been undermined, but there is nothing definite to take its place (p. 132).

School also means that the child has less time for play. When he returns home in the afternoon he has many responsibilities which he must fulfill in order to pay his parents back for the school fees they provide. With the older children in school the youngest has no one to look after and play with him. Welbourn summarized the life of a child in Buganda as a "serious and often keenly competitive preparation for life" (p. 130). While many families have been able to combine the new way of life with the traditional, many others have not yet been successful in providing the child with a stable framework in which he can learn about himself and the world around him.

A. R. Wandira (1961) described traditional education and the influences on it within various tribes in Uganda, and related it to Western education in structure and contribution. The influences on it are: (1) the past, which is presented to the child through legends, myths, proverbs, riddles, and songs which justify the existing social order and reinforce customs; (2) the family and clan, which act as models of expected behavior; (3) the village, which presents a wide variety of situations calling for prescribed behavior; (4) economic considerations related to the income of the community; (5) the political structure; and (6) the philosophical and religious systems which provide a base for the values and beliefs of the society.

Traditional education as described by Wandira, Fortes (1938), and Raum (1940) does not develop sharp distinctions between the adult's and the child's minds. The emphasis is on learning by doing rather than by teaching, and there is no departmentalization of curriculum. In traditional societies education and life are co-determined (Wandria, p. 165), and while society provides support for traditional education, it does not provide such support for Western education.

The lack of support for Western education within traditional cultures was also discussed by Verhaegen and Laroche (1958) and Valantin and Collomb (1962), all of whom suggest that there is little correspondence between the traditional culture and the formal school system. Both sets of authors also describe problems that the African child has upon entering school. One of great import is that the child has limited pre-school experiences, which means that he frequently enters school without the experiences necessary for Western education. His range of knowledge is limited and it cannot be assumed that he can begin learning in the same way and on the same level that the Western child can. A second is that frequently the language of the school may not be the child's mother tongue. Thus, besides coping with a new system, he must also learn a new language and learn to function abstractly in it. A third is that the content of school programs is largely irrelevant to the child. Currently, the primary school is designed for the child who will continue through the entire system. This means that for the vast majority of the school population, whose formal education ends after primary school, the curriculum does little to prepare them for their future. Verhaegen (1960) described the child at the end of primary school as one who lacks integration and exhibits intellectual fragmentation and a kind of instability. Basically, his introduction to Western values has been incomplete, and when he leaves school he belongs neither to the traditional way of life nor to the Western world. (This problem of acculturation will be discussed further in the fourth part of this chapter.)

As early as 1938 O. Liesenborghs, in the Congo, realized that teaching in Africa raises special problems which require special solutions. The knowledge collected about the African peoples to that date indicated to the author the need for revised teaching methods. Liesenborghs refuted the idea that what is good education in the West is directly applicable to Africa, and called for a psychological understanding of the Africans and an adjustment in teaching accordingly.

P. O. Duminy (1965, 1967) approached the problem of education in Africa from the standpoint of educational psychology. He discussed the development of educational theory to illustrate that it is necessary to know what a child's understanding and attitude are toward objects in order to know how to structure the material presented to him. This led Duminy to point out the importance of being aware of the subtleties of a culture in order to understand the effects of the physical and cultural environment in which the learner is placed. To illustrate some of these considerations, Duminy listed three things that a teacher in a Bantu culture must be aware of: (1) the gap between the school and home environment; (2) the difficulties of two-dimensional perception (frequently the child lacks concrete references for words he appears to know and understand); and (3) the degree of motivation of the child, for the child has strong natural interests that should be used as a basis to stimulate other interests (1965, pp. 12-13).

Donald Munro (1966) emphasized the importance of home support to education. At the present time there is only a small middle class in Africa which provides the child with pre-school and after-school instruction. The project Munro worked on attempted to look at the trends of development in Africa in terms of (1) the intellectual stimulation of the child, together with the availability of opportunities for self-stimulation, and (2) some of the determinants of motivational patterns which are important to education and development. Munro is currently looking at child-rearing practices as they apply to these two areas.

P. Chike Onwuachi (1966) discussed how a new cultural pattern is emerging within Africa which includes indigenous traditions as well as new values significant to the culture (pp. 289-292). Joseph Kizerbo (1966) sees education as a "galvanizer of African values" which should be based on an infrastructure of African cultures (p. 235). He also discusses how such subjects as philosophy, geography, history, language, and the arts need to be re-examined in order to include the contributions of indigenous cultures.

Recent authors have called for a combination of traditional and Western values and methods to produce a new educational system. As Read (1959) has pointed out, education is used both to perpetuate a culture and to change it. In designing an educational system there must be a balance between cultural change and cultural continuity (p. 167).

John Gay and Michael Cole (1967) undertook a study of the Kpelle tribe in Liberia to understand the existing culture in all its facets, and to develop an educational system based on the knowledge, concepts, and experience provided by the existing system. Through the use of tests, many of which were devised on the basis of an understanding of tribal tradition, the authors obtained a comprehensive picture of traditionally learned concepts and abilities. They then provided recommendations for making the formal school a situation where a child can enlarge the world in which he lives. They felt that it is important to provide a different approach to education so that the child can "retain as much as possible of his cultural heritage. He must not become simply a poor imitation of an American or European child. He must *not* lose his identity" (p. 96). Their book is an excellent example of how a culture should be studied.

SOCIALIZATION: ITS EFFECTS ON PERSONALITY

> Faults are like a hill, you mount on your own and then see other peoples'.
>
> Hausa Proverb

The socialization process is broader in scope than the events involved in child rearing and the educational system. As the child grows he finds his role in society through contact with the total social system of which he is a member. This section provides a discussion of socializing forces within various African cultures, and their hypothesized effects on the development of the total personality.

A study by Gustav Jahoda (1954) illustrates the effect that a child's relationships with his society can have on his self-image. Jahoda became interested in the names given to children in the Ashanti tribe. Traditionally, part of the child's name included the name for the day of the week on which he was born, each weekday having a personality type associated with it. For example, those born on Monday (Kwadwo) are thought to be retiring, quiet, and peaceful in nature. Those born on Wednesday (Kwaku) are characterized by a quick temper and aggressiveness, and are thought to be trouble-makers. Jahoda found that the tendency to expect children to act in accordance with these names is prevalent, even among the educated.

Jahoda then looked at the official records of delinquency and found that those born on Monday got into trouble significantly less often than those born on Wednesday. By looking at the type of offenses committed, Jahoda found that those born on Wednesday committed offenses of an aggressive nature significantly more than those born on other days of the week. He concluded that the child gets a picture of what he is from his society. The child also apparently learns his sex role through contact with adults in his society. The work done by Herbert Barry, Margaret Bacon, and Irvin Child (1957, 1959) on the cross-cultural sex differences in socialization indicates that they are a result of the cultural milieu, rather than being biological in nature. Their analyses of various cultures indicate that people vary in the degree to which differentiations are made between the sexes. This differentiation is affected by the type of economy of the group. For example, an economy that places a high premium on superior strength of the male would be one involved in hunting large animals, keeping large stock, and growing grain rather than root crops (1959). Secondly, this differentiation is affected by the type of living group found. If a nuclear family lives alone, less differentiation of role is found because the males and females have to be able to take the other's role in case of sickness or merely to do the necessary work (1957, p. 32).

Jahoda (1956b), in addition to looking at self-images in children, studied sex differences in socialization. He gave individuals a shape preference test and analyzed it in psychoanalytic terms. He predicted that in a culture where there is less sex repression, one would expect sex differences to be smaller. He found that the sex differences in the group tested were greatly reduced but still significantly different.

It has been hypothesized that as children learn to relate to the world, they go through a period of animism. Studies have been done cross-culturally to see to what extent this animism is affected by the socialization processes within a given culture. Jahoda (1958a, b, c) looked at the presence of animism in children of primary and middle school age in West Africa. The children were told a story and asked about the causality involved. They were then asked to explain where the music comes from in a gramophone. The results indicate that animism becomes progressively less important as children grow older. Also, there was less animism connected with the gramophone. Jahoda hypothesized that this is because the gramophone is not a part of the traditional culture, and that people accept "Western technology" without giving it animistic characteristics. (1958b, p. 220)

In the tribal group studied by Jahoda, language factors influence animism in that many words have a "strong" form. The use of this form indicates the presence of animistic powers. For this reason the object involved in the story was one which did not have a strong form. Thus, responses corresponded to the modes of thinking rather than conventional linguistic use (1958b, p. 222). Using the same story, Jahoda (1958c) also looked at the West African's ideas of imminent justice and hypothesized that the beliefs shown were a direct result of parental teaching. According to Jahoda, in modern societies the individual becomes decreasingly dependent on adult constraints and intellectually and morally autonomous. In societies which are closely knit, such practices as initiation do not liberate the individual, but "place him under the overwhelming moral constraints of the elders" (p. 245). Jahoda believed it was possible to grade cultures according to the degree of moral constraint present.

A study currently in progress is being conducted by Orlando Jones, who is looking at the development of moral judgment in African, Indian, and European children in Southern Rhodesia. He is using a series of tests derived from Piaget's work on the moral development of the child in an attempt to see if Piaget's stages are evident in all three races and at what ages the stages occur. The experiment was begun in 1961 and proposed to last three or four years.

Mary Lystad (1960b) attempted to assess the traditional values of Ghanaian children through an analysis of their stories and paintings. On one occasion she had students write the traditional story they liked best. They were also to tell how old they were when they first heard it, what language it was told in, and who told it to them. At a second session the students were to write a story about a contemporary boy or girl living in their same town. A content analysis of the traditional stories revealed concerns about material needs which were largely unsatisfied. The stories were enjoyed because of the morals, which emphasized the necessity of doing good to others. The children's own stories presented a picture of a less barren life. Individuals in the stories were not worried about physical needs and had more time to enjoy human companionship. The characters achieved satisfaction from their pursuits and were better able to choose means consonant with the ends desired. Lystad concluded that due to the changes in the life of Ghanaian society, children's "thinking has shifted somewhat from that of their parents" (p. 462).

To what extent does socialization affect personality development? In an attempt to answer this question S. F. Nadel (1937) did two experiments among the Yoruba and the Nupe of Nigeria. The first required an African to repeat a story that was told to him. This he did twice, once later the same day and again in one week. The second part of the experiment was for students to look at six pictures, after which they were asked to write a description of them. They were asked to do this again a week later, but were not shown the pictures a second time. From this experiment, Nadel concluded that the Yoruba, who have a highly developed realistic image-art, drama, and religious system, stress rational elements, logical cohesion, and a strongly pronounced meaning-oriented approach to observational data. The Nupe, whose beliefs revolve around abstract, impersonal magical principles, are more\detached and more sensitive to spatial and temporal arrangement. The Nupe stress unity and the emotional tone in the situation, rather than the facts of meaning and rational consistency emphasized by the Yoruba. Nadel attributed this psychological orientation to the differences between the tribal cultures (p. 210).

L. Haward and W. Roland (1954, 1955a, b) used the Goodenough Draw-A-Man Test with Nigerians and Europeans in an attempt to assess the personality characteristics of Nigerians. Although the authors stated that this test, which has been standardized on a Western culture, does not represent the "real" personality profile of the natives, the authors proceeded to draw the following conclusion from the low test score of the Nigerians. The pictures drawn by Nigerians, they found, indicated a lack of individualization in the culture, and a basically rigid and concrete attitude toward life (1954). In a second experiment, they compared Nigerian children's drawings with those done by schizophrenics. They concluded that the results "suggest the existence of certain psychological mechanisms or frames of thought which [the African] appears to share with the White mental patient" (1955a, p. 28). In their concluding article (1955b), the authors stated that the results do not show an inferiority, but an undeveloped ability to abstract or synthesize. The authors hypothesized that, as a result of child-rearing practices within the society, the African fails to develop a self-image which is distinct from the rest of reality. The cultural conflict arising between the traditional and contemporary life produces an individual who is trying to make the best of two possible worlds. This situation develops mental processes in the African analogous to the split mind of the schizophrenic (p. 42).

Another technique which has been used to study the personality of the African is a Thematic Apperception Test (TAT). One of the first individuals to develop a TAT for Africans was Ombredane (1954), working in the Congo, whose work was concerned more with the development of the technique than with a systematic study of the Congolese peoples. Ombredane discussed his results in some detail. He coined the phrase "musico-choreographic" to describe the Congolese personality. The Western mind, in contrast, was termed "arithmo-geometrical."

M. Leblanc (1958), who did a considerable amount of work to develop a TAT for the Congolese African, was quite critical of the pictures by Ombredane, in that they presented a world of fantasy rather than of reality. Rather than using a Belgian artist, as Ombredane did, Leblanc worked with a Congolese artist to develop a set of fifteen pictures based on a Bantu point of view. Leblanc's pictures were first used with women from two tribes in the Congo – one quite traditional, the other urban and more Westernized. The pictures were designed to study the women's attitudes about parental and tribal relations and cross-sex and same-sex relationships. From the results, Leblanc discussed the personality traits of the two tribal groups represented.

Marie Knapen (1958, 1962) looked at a Bacongo society and related its socialization processes to the personality development of the child. She compared Western society with the Bacongo society in terms of six characteristics. First, in Western society emphasis is placed on searching for indivdual values, while in the Bacongo society social values are sought. Second, the child in the Bacongo society has a realistic education, characterized by participation in real-life tasks. On the other hand, the Westerner takes part in a detached educational system which involves abstract ideas. Third, whereas discipline appeals to the personal aspiration level of the Western child, it appeals to the social duty of the Bacongo. Fourth, Western society encourages the child to "grow up," while in the Bacongo society there is a feeling of certainty that nature looks after normal growth. Fifth, while the Bacongo society stresses maintenance of the norm, Western cultures place emphasis on the unique and exceptional in the individual. Sixth, the Western individual has intense affective ties within a constricted group, a heightened level of consciousness of self, a sense of responsibility, a regular occurrence of feelings of guilt, a feeling of independence, and a spirit of individualism. The individual in the Bacongo society has affective relations of low intensity with a large number of people, a relatively weak consciousness of self, a preponderance of fear of others rather than a sense of guilt, intense feelings of dependence, and a collective spirit (1958, pp. 228-229).

Whereas Knapen studied only one cultural group, the broader relationship between personality development and cultural setting was looked at by Whiting and Child (1953). Rather than describing in detail the life pattern of one culture, they attempted to test general hypotheses across cultures. Two aspects of socialization the authors analyzed in psycho-analytic and behavior theory terms were child-rearing practices and the attitudes toward illness. Whereas child-rearing practices are universal in that all parents deal with the same type problems (e.g., infant care, toilet training, and weaning), each society has developed a characteristic way of handling them.

Whiting and Child looked at the oral, anal, sexual, and dependence systems of behavior, and rated them on three facets: (1) the initial indulgence, (2) the age at which socialization begins, and (3) the severity of the socialization (pp.

67-68). The authors saw these systems as playing a large part in personality processes which mediate between the culture which produces them and the culture which is perpetuated. From their work, Whiting and Child concluded that the general notion that cultural integration is achieved through personality processes is valid. They also felt that there are some concepts of personality development which hold true universally.

In order to understand why cultures foster different personality processes, Barry, Child, and Bacon (1959) looked at socialization as it related to the economic system within the culture. They hypothesized that the emphasis in socialization will be toward the development of behavior especially useful to the adult economy. If, as the authors suggest, the economic role tends to be generalized to the rest of behavior, predictions might be made about the typical character development of adults in different subsistence economies. The authors looked at training for obedience, responsibility, nurturance, achievement, self-reliance, and general independence, and rated 500 societies on these dimensions.

Barry, Child, and Bacon then summarized their findings by saying that pressures for obedience and responsibility are found in cultures with high-accumulation economies whose food supply must be protected and developed gradually throughout the year. On the other hand, "pressures toward self-reliance and achievement should shape the child into ... independent adults who can take initiative in [gathering] food daily from nature and thus ensure survival in societies with a low-accumulation economy" (p. 62).

The occupational aspirations of various African peoples have been studied by researchers. One such was compiled by Rémi Clignet (1964), who studied the works of several individuals and institutions on the occupational aspirations and motivations of elementary and secondary school pupils in the West African countries of Senegal, Gabon, Ivory Coast, and Mali. The results indicated that, for the most part, African pupils are realistic in their choice of future occupations. Clignet suggested that pupils' choices of bureaucratic positions reflect the European tendency for the promise of social mobility. Also, the data reflect the cultural heritage. For example, Senegalese pupils were oriented toward the family unit, and mentioned the necessity of providing for those in their family. The data also indicated significant differences within all four countries between the sexes in choice of occupation and motivation. Males saw themselves in positions of authority over the family and related their future occupations to the social group (family, region, nation). Females, on the other hand, were more individualistic and did not relate to social units. Males saw their education as a way to efficiently get themselves into the functioning society, but education did not appear to affect the status of females.

Clignet expressed concern over the fact that agriculture was chosen as a future occupation by only a few of the pupils. Also, the range of occupations chosen by the subjects was very limited. This seemed to be a result of both a limited labor market and the lack of adequate information about jobs available. Clignet placed the blame on the schools, which he felt inadequately prepare the child for his adult life.

Robert LeVine (1964, 1966) did a study of achievement motivation among the Hausa, Yoruba, and Ibo in Nigeria. The questions being explored were: (1) Are there measurable differences in personality in culturally different populations? (2) If so, what are the socio-cultural causes of these differences? and (3) What are the social consequences of these differences?

From an understanding of the cultures of the tribes, LeVine hypothesized that his study would show that the Hausa have the greatest resistance to mobility and, therefore, will exhibit the least achievement motivation; that the Ibo are traditionally occupation oriented and the most mobile, and will exhibit the greatest amount of achievement motivation; and that the Yoruba will be intermediary.

LeVine's study was done with fifth and sixth form pupils (Hausa-65Ss, Northern Yoruba-33Ss, Southern Yoruba-106Ss, Ibo-138Ss) ranging in age from 15 to 28. To assess the degree of the pupils' "need achievement" ($\underline{n}$), LeVine did an analysis of dreams. He asked pupils to report both their most recent and most recurrent dreams. He concluded that traditional patterns, rather than the level of parents' education, religious affiliation, examination anxiety, or physiological drive, determine the degree of need achievement within the three tribes studied. The rank order of tribes on need achievement was as predicted (1964, pp. 93-94). LeVine did several subsidiary studies to further explore the above results. He concluded his work (1966) with a discussion of alternative hypotheses which suggested other variables which may have had an effect on the results, and he outlined studies which should be done to test them.

Corahann Okorodudu (1966) related the effects of the existing culture on achievement motivation among the Kpelle of Liberia. Her work begins with a thorough and objective description of socialization within the tribe. In her research, she compared three types of households: polygynous, nuclear, and mother-child. She also considered the differences which might occur as a result of father absence, marital status of the mother, and the household shifts of the child due to adoption. Some of Okorodudu's results indicated that children from homes where the father is present (nuclear) have higher need achievement ($\underline{n}$), whereas those whose fathers are absent have low $\underline{n}$. The children of a monogamous mother have a higher $\underline{n}$ than the children of a polygynous mother. It is interesting to note that in polygynous families, the children of the second wife scored higher than those of the first.

Okorodudu hypothesized that boys in nuclear families are preoccupied with achievement because they are striving to achieve the status of the boy from the polygynous family. (In the Kpelle tribe polygynous families have the highest social and economic prestige). However, the boy in the polygynous family strives only to fit into the existing framework, since his family has already attained status. Due to the large number of members in the polygynous household, competition is perceived as disruptive and there is a low emphasis on overt achievement. In a polygynous family a boy's maturity means that he must take on the responsibility of the large family. Thus, he frequently remains a "child" as long as he can (pp. 257-271).

The above illustrate only some of the hypotheses offered by Okorodudu. Her work has many implications for those interested in the problems of education in a culture where motivations may be quite different from those found in Western societies.

ACCULTURATION

When a fool does not succeed in bleaching ebony he tries to blacken ivory.

Amharic Proverb

In the book they edited, *Continuity and Change in African Cultures,* William Bascom and Melville Herskovits (1959) discussed the idea that "There is no African culture which has not been affected in some way by European contact, and there is none which has entirely given way before it" (p. 3). They also felt that societies differ in their acculturation level — to the degree to which they adopt Western ideas — and pointed out that the acculturation process is additive, rather than substitutive, and is selective. A child's socialization, they said, is influenced by the acculturation level of his society.

In an attempt to look at the degree of acculturation of Ghanaian children, Lystad asked some to draw a picture for her without stating what subject she wanted them to draw. She then did a content analysis of the pictures, and interpreted them as a reflection of the child's feelings about his universe. Although these children were city dwellers, the pictures depicted rural life. The major activity portrayed was that of food-gathering. The only political scenes included were traditional, and the then-current national politics were ignored. The pictures were realistic in their portrayal of traditional life and showed a rational orientation to life. Lystad concluded that the traditional emphasis shown in these pictures may indicate that social change is not occurring as rapidly as thought by Western observers. Perhaps, she hypothesized, individuals are largely satisfied by and identify with their traditional culture (1960a, p. 241). One question about this analysis that might be asked is: to what extent do the experiences these children might have had with drawing various scenes, rather than their feelings about the universe, influence their choice of subject matter in such a situation?

Jahoda (1959) was also interested in the degree of acculturation of Ghanaians. To assess this, he looked at the national stereotypes they displayed and their preferences for peoples of various nationalities. Through interviews with 214 adults of varying levels of education, Jahoda found that their rankings of nationalities were similar to those of Western people. However, the Ghanaians tended to do more stereotyping and their choices were more radically divergent than those of Europeans. Jahoda hypothesized that the similarity was due to the educational system, which transmits Western values (p. 174).

Biesheuvel (1955) was interested in looking at the attitudes Africans in South Africa had toward the Western standards of conduct being imposed on them. He found that there was considerable individual difference in the endorsement of Western attitudes, and that the rank of opinions relating to each attitude was dependent on the specific nature of the situation, not the result of stereotyping. In a follow-up of that study, Biesheuvel concluded that "as a group respondents were not motivated by a desire to give 'approved' answers but that their replies reflected an inwardly accepting value system" (1959a, p. 155). The educated African has a thorough appreciation of the moral and legal codes of Western cultures in South Africa, and wholeheartedly indentifies himself with both the ethical and religious values except in matters of man's natural needs and beliefs about witchcraft. In these latter areas tradition persists. An interesting comment by Biesheuvel was that he found "no evidence of a growth of hostility toward the European" (p. 154).

Marshall Segall (1963) did a study among the Banyankole in Uganda to assess the extent to which they acquire the attitudes and opinions of Europeans with whom they are in contact. He was looking particularly at how far Africans acquiesce and take on negative attitudes that the Europeans have about them. Subjects (68 Africans and 28 Europeans) were presented with a series of 32 statements about the Banyankole peoples, and for each statement the subjects were to choose one of four responses: strongly agree, agree, disagree, strongly disagree. The statements were presented verbally to the Africans by the European investigator, and the Africans replied verbally. The Europeans were sent the questionnaire through the mail and responded in written form; they were never required to confront the investigator with their responses.

In discussing the results, Segall described, quite extensively, the methodological difficulties encountered during the study. Taking these into consideration, the results suggest that (a) few Africans take on the anti-African feelings of Europeans, and (b) those who do are probably only acquiescing with anti-African statements because these were presented to them by a European. Segall termed this "superficial acquiescence," as distinguished from what other researchers have described as Africans' "profound indentification" with European attitudes. Considering the methodological difficulties which may affect results, Segall suggested that, in looking at the results of similar studies, researchers should be aware of the response styles of the respondents — whether they be European or from other cultures — before attempting to discuss the results of studies on acculturation.

The impact of acculturation and its effects on the further development of a society is the subject of Doob's book, *Becoming More Civilized: A Psychological Exploration* (1960a). In it, Doob summarized the research to date, and then made a series of hypotheses about cultures in the process of changing from traditional to new ways. These hypotheses suggest many areas that need more adequate research, and show the inadequacy of our present knowledge of the African. In another discussion of the psychological problems facing Africans exposed to two opposing socialization processes, Doob (1960b) concluded that in order to facilitate the process of change the immediate situation must alter. Individuals must learn to extend both their interests and their knowledge. They must also learn to abandon immediate rewards and, more difficult still, they must be able to abandon some of the certainties which traditional society provides.

M. Badri and W. Dennis (1964), like Haward and Roland whose studies were discussed earlier, used the Draw-A-Man test with Africans. Instead of interpreting the results in terms of a personality difference between the African and the European, Badri and Dennis used the test to show the degree of Westernization of African children. They hypothesized that children in greater contact with the modern way of life would draw men in Western dress, whereas children either unacquainted with Western man or who held negative attitudes toward modernization, would draw a man in more primitive dress. Badri and Dennis concluded from the work of Haward and Roland (1954, 1955a, b) that Nigerians were identifying with the more traditional figure rather than with the more Westernized man.

To look at the acculturation level of various African tribes, Leonard and Mary Ainsworth (1962) did a series of studies with students in secondary schools in Uganda and Kenya. In one study they used projective techniques to assess the political awareness of students and their attitudes toward authority. They found that the more acculturated African is more frequently frustrated, and thus more hostile and aggressive toward authority figures. But he also has more effective means of handling his frustration and aggression. The authors also found that students in Uganda were more politically aware, more actively discontent with the status quo, and more nationalistic than those in Kenya (1962a, b). One can raise the question whether these attitudes may be attributed wholly to acculturation or whether they are not perhaps linked with the traditional system of government and the current political situation in the country.

In a third analysis, the Ainsworths discovered that the degree of acculturation has less effect upon students' attitudes toward parents than it does upon personality characteristics, for many of their attitudes toward parents remain consistent with the traditional attitudes of the cultures. The more acculturated students place a higher value on education and tend to view teachers more positively than do the less acculturated students (1962c).

In summarizing their work with these students, the Ainsworths stated that "nearly all the differences between schools in this study seem attributable to the difference in the general level of acculturation" (1962d, p. 424). In some cases, however, the authors indicate that the difference is attributable to the cultures represented. Also, some of the differences are the result of the specific acculturation received at the school (e.g., a school run by Catholics would produce a different pattern of living from one operated by the government). The authors felt that those studied did not seem to be experiencing a high degree of stress due to cultural conflict. Rather, there was a general acceptance of the acculturation process.

BIBLIOGRAPHY

Ainsworth, Leonard. "Rigidity, Stress and Acculturation." *Journal of Social Psychology,* 1959, *49*, pp. 131-136.

————, and Ainsworth, Mary "Acculturation in East Africa: I. Political Awareness and Attitudes about Authority." *Journal of Social Psychology,* 1962a, *57*, pp. 391-399.

————. "Acculturation in East Africa: II. Frustration and Aggression." *Journal of Social Psychology,* 1962b, *57*, pp. 401-407.

————. "Acculturation in East Africa: III. Attitudes towards Parents, Teachers and Education." *Journal of Social Psychology,* 1962c, *57*, pp. 409-415.

————. "Acculturation in East Africa: IV. Summary and Discussion." *Journal of Social Psychology,* 1962d, *57*, pp. 417-432.

Ainsworth, Mary. *The Development of Infant-Mother Interaction among the Ganda.* Unpublished paper read at a meeting of the Tavistock Group on Mother-Infant Interaction, London, 1961.

————. *Infancy in Uganda: Infant Care and Growth of Love.* Baltimore: Johns Hopkins Press, 1967.

Albino, R. C., and Thompson, V. J. "The Effects of Sudden Weaning on Zulu Children." *British Journal of Medical Psychology,* 1956, *29*, pp. 177-210.

Badri, M., and Dennis, W. "Human Figure Drawings in Relation to Modernization in Sudan." *Journal of Psychology,* 1964, *58*, pp. 421-425.

Barrington-Kaye. *Bringing Up Children in Ghana: An Impressionistic Survey.* London: George Allen & Unwin, 1962.

Barry, Herbert, Bacon, Margaret, and Child, Irvin. "A Cross-Cultural Survey of Some Sex Differences in Socialization." *Journal of Abnormal and Social Psychology,* 1957, *55*, pp. 327-332.

56

————. "Relation of Child Training to Subsistence Economy." *American Anthropologist,* 1959, *61*, pp. 51-63.

Bascom, William, and Herskovits, Melville (eds.). *Continuity and Change in African Cultures.* Chicago: University of Chicago Press, 1959.

Biesheuvel, Simon. "The Measurement of African Attitudes toward European Ethnical Concepts, Custom, Law and Administration of Justice." *Journal of the National Institute of Personnel Research,* 1955, *6*, pp. 5-17.

————. "Aspects of Africa: II. The Abilities of Africans." *Listener,* 1956, *55*, pp. 447-449.

————. "Methodology in the Study of Attitudes of Africans." *Journal of Social Psychology,* 1958, *47*, pp. 169-184.

————. "Further Studies on the Measurement of Attitudes towards Western Ethical Concepts." *Journal of the National Institute of Personnel Research,* 1959a, *7* (3), pp. 141-155.

————. *Race, Culture and Personality.* Johannesburg: South African Institute of Race Relations, 1959b.

Bricklin, B., and Zeleznik, C. "A Psychological Investigation of Selected Ethiopian Adolescents by Means of Rorschach and Other Projective Tests." *Human Organization,* 1963-4, *22*, pp. 291-303.

Busia, K. A. *Purposeful Education in Africa.* The Hague: Moulton, 1964.

Carothers, J. C. *The African Mind in Health and Disease: A Study in Ethno-Psychiatry.* Geneva: WHO, 1953.

————. *The Psychology of MauMau.* Nairobi: Government Printing Office, 1954.

Castle, E. B. *Growing Up in East Africa.* London: Oxford University Press, 1966.

Centner, T. "L'Enfant Africain et Ses Jeux: Dans le Cadre de la Vie Traditionnel au Katanga." *Collection Mémoires C.E.S.P.I.* 17°, 1962.

Clignet, Rémi. "Éducation et Aspirations Professionnelles." *Tiers-Monde,* 1964, *5* (whole No. 17).

Dean, R. F. A. "Health Education and Protein-Calorie Malnutrition." *Journal of Tropical Medicine,* 1962.

Delbard, B. *Étude de Quelques Déséquilibres Crées par l'Industrie au Togo: Contribution à l'Étude Sociologique des Problèmes du Travail en Afrique Noire.* PARIS: École de Psychologues Practiciens, 1962.

Denis, F. "L'Enseignement Traditionnel au Congo Avant l'Arrivée des Blancs." *La Revue Nouvelle.,* 1951, *1*(4), pp. 346-355.

DeRidder, J. C. *The Personality of the Urban African in South Africa.* London: Routledge & Kegan Paul, 1961.

Desamais, R., and Gineste, R. *Face aux Enfants.* Paris, Collection Bourrelier, Librairie Armand Colin, 1963.

Doob, Leonard. "An Introduction into the Psychology of Acculturation." *Journal of Social Psychology,* 1957a, *45*, pp. 143-160.

————. "Psychological Research in Nonliterate Societies." *American Psychologist,* 1957b, *12*, pp. 756-758.

————. *Becoming More Civilized: A Psychological Exploration.* New Haven: Yale University Press, 1960a.

————. "The Psychological Pressure upon Modern Africans." *Journal of Human Relations,* 1960b, *8*(3 & 4), pp. 465-472.

————. "Psychology." In R. A. Lystad (ed.). *The African World: A Survey of Social Research.* London: Pall Mall Press, 1965, pp. 373-415 and 543-549.

Duminy, P. A. *Learning and the African Child.* Pretoria: Fort Hare University Press, 1965.

————(ed.). *Trends and Challenges in the Education of the South African Bantu.* Pretoria: Fort Hare University Press, 1967.

Ferron, Oscar. *A Study of Certain Factors Affecting the Tested Intelligence of Some Groups of West African Children.* Unpublished doctoral dissertation, London University, 1964.

Fortes, Meyer. *Social and Psychological Aspects of Education in Taleland.* London: Oxford University Press for the International Institute of African Languages and Cultures, 1938.

Foster, Philip. "Status, Power and Education in a Traditional Community." *School Review,* 1964, *72*, pp. 158-182.

Fox, Lorene. "Learning Adventure in East Africa." *Childhood Education,* 1965, *41*, pp. 343-348.

————. *East African Childhood: Three Versions.* Nairobi, Kenya: Oxford University Press, 1967.

Gay, John, and Cole, Michael. *The New Mathematics and an Old Culture: A Study of Learning among the Kpelle of Liberia.* New York: Holt, Rinehart and Winston, 1967.

Haward, L. R. C. "Extra-Cultural Differences in Drawings of the Human Figure by African Children." *Ethnos,* 1956, *3-4*, pp. 220-230.

————, and Roland, W. A. "Some Intercultural Differences on the Draw-A-Man Test: I. Goodenough Scores." *Man,* 1954, *54*, pp. 86-88.

————. "Some Intercultural Differences on the Draw-A-Man Test: II. Machover Series." *Man,* 1955a, *55*, pp. 27-29.

————. "Some Intercultural Differences on the Draw-A-Man Test: III. Conclusion." *Man,* 1955b, *55*, pp. 40-42.

Health Education and the Mother and Child in East Africa. *Journal of Tropical Medicine and Hygiene,* 1962.

Hellmann, Ellen. *Problems of Urban Bantu Youth.* Johannesburg: South African Institute of Race Relations, 1940.

Henderson, R. H., and Henderson, H. K. *An Outline of Traditional Onitsha Ibo Socialization.* Ibadan: Institute of Education, University College, Ibadan, Occasional Paper No. 5, 1966.

Herskovits, Melville. "Critique on Carothers' Book, The African Mind in Health and Disease." *Man,* 1954, *56*(26), pp. 30-31.

————. "The African Cultural Background in the Modern Scene." In C. G. Haines (ed.). *Africa Today.* Baltimore: Johns Hopkins Press, 1955.

————. *The Human Factor in Changing Africa.* New York: Knopf, 1962.

Huizinga, J. *Homo Ludens: A Study of the Play-Element in Culture.* Boston: Beacon Press, 1960.

58

Jahoda, Gustav. "A Note on Ashanti Names and Their Relationship to Personality." *British Journal of Psychology*, 1954, *45*, pp. 192-195.

—————. "Assessment of Abstract Behavior in a Non-Western Culture." *Journal of Abnormal and Social Psychology*, 1956a, *53*, pp. 237-243.

—————. "Sex Differences in Preferences for Shapes: A Cross-Cultural Replication." *British Journal of Psychology*, 1956b, *47*, pp. 126-132.

—————. "Child Animism: I. A Critical Survey of Cross-Cultural Research." *Journal of Social Psychology*, 1958a, *47*, pp. 197-212.

—————. "Child Animism: II. A Study in West Africa." *Journal of Social Psychology*, 1958b, *47* pp. 213-222.

—————. "Immanent Justice among West African Children." *Journal of Social Psychology*, 1958c, *47*, pp. 241-248.

—————. "Nationality Preference and National Stereotypes in Ghana Before Independence." *Journal of Social Psychology*, 1959, *50*, pp. 165-174.

Jones, Orlando. *The Development of Moral Judgment in a Sample of African, Indian and European School Children in Southern Rhodesia.* Unpublished masters thesis, in progress.

Kidd, Dudley. *Savage Childhood: A Study of Kafir Children.* London: Adam and Charles Black, 1906.

Kimenye, Barbara. *Kalasandra.* London: Oxford University Press, 1965.

Kizerbo, Joseph. "Cultural Cohesion Through Education." In John Hanson and C. S. Brembeck (eds.). *Education and the Development of Nations.* New York: Holt, Rinehart, and Winston, 1966.

Klineberg, Otto. *Race Differences.* New York: Harper & Bros., 1935.

Knapen, Marie. "Some Results of an Enquiry into the Influence of Child Training Practices on the Development of Personality in a Bacongo Society (Belgian Congo)." *Journal of Social Psychology*, 1958, *47*, pp. 223-229.

—————. *L'Enfant Mukongo.* Paris: Publications Universitaires de Louvain, Editions Beatrice – Nauwelaerts, 1962.

Laird, A. J. *Psychological Research Carried Out During the Period April – December, 1953.* East African Institute of Social Research Paper, No. 54, 1954.

Leblanc, M. "Adaptation Africaine et Comparison Interculturelle d'une Épreuve Projective: Test de Rosenzweig." *Revue de Psychologie Appliqué,* 1956, *6*(2), pp. 91-110.

—————. "La Problématique de l'Adaptation du TAT au Congo." *Zaire,* 1958, *12*(4), pp. 339-348.

LeVine, Barbara. *Yoruba Students' Memories of Childhood Rewards and Punishments.* Institute of Education, University College, Ibadan, Occasional Publication No. 2, 1962.

LeVine, Robert. "Africa." In F. K. L. Hsu (ed.). *Psychological Anthropology: Approaches to Culture and Personality.* Homewood, Illinois: Dorsay Press, 1961.

—————. "Child Rearing in Sub-Saharan Africa: An Interim Report." *Menninger Clinic Bulletin,* 1963, *27*, pp. 245-256.

—————. *Achievement Motivation in Nigeria: A Study of Personality and Social Structure.* University of Chicago, 1964 (mimeo).

————. *Dreams and Deeds: Achievement Motivation in Nigeria.* Chicago: University of Chicago Press, 1966.

————, and LeVine, Barbara "Studying Child Rearing and Personality Development in an East African Community." *Annals of the New York Academy of Science,* 1962, *96*, pp. 620-628.

————. "Nyansongo: A Gusii Community in Kenya." In Beatrice Whiting (ed.). *Six Cultures: Studies of Child Rearing.* New York: John Wiley and Sons, Inc., 1963.

Liddicoat, Renée. and Koza, Constance. "Language Development in African Infants." *Psychologica Africana,* 1963, *10*, pp. 108-116.

Liesenborghs, O. "Naar een Afrikaanse Opouedkunde." *Kongo-Overze* (Antwerpen), 1938, pp. 1-16.

Lystad, Mary. "Paintings of Ghanaian Children." *Africa,* 1960a, *30*, pp. 238-242.

————. "Traditional Values of Ghanaian Children." *American Anthropoligist,* 1960b, *62*, pp. 454-464.

Marwick, M. G. "Mr. Ritchie's Double Hypothesis." *Rhodes-Livingstone Journal,* 1949, *2*, pp. 69-76.

Miller, N. *The Child in Primitive Society.* London: Kegan Paul, Trench, Trubner & Co., Ltd., 1928.

Mujunga, A. B. *Punishing Children to Make Them Learn (in Uganda).* Kampala, Uganda: Uganda Publishing House, 1967.

Munro, Donald. "Environment and the Intellectual Growth of Pre-School Urban African Children." *Bulletin of the Institute of Social Research.* (University of Zambia), 1966, *1*, pp. 31-36.

Nadel, S. F. "A Field Experiment in Racial Psychology." *British Journal of Psychology,* 1937, *28*, pp. 195-211.

Nyerere, Julius K. *Education for Self-Reliance.* Dar es Salaam: Information Services Division, Ministry of Information and Tourism, 1966.

Okorodudu, Corahann. *Achievement Training and Motivation among the Kpelle of Liberia: A Study of Household Structure Antecedents.* Unpublished doctoral dissertation, Harvard University, 1966.

Ombredane, André, "L'Exploration de la Mentalité des Noirs Congolais au Moyen d'une Epreuve Projective: Le Congo TAT." *Mémoires de l'Institut Royal Colonial Blege, Section des Sciences Naturelles et Medicinales,* 1954, *37*(5), p. 41.

Ominde, Simeon H. *The Luo Girl from Infancy to Marriage.* London: Macmillan and Co., Ltd., 1952.

Onwauchi, P. Chike. "African Traditional Culture and Western Education." *Journal of Negro Education,* 1966, *35*, pp. 289-292.

Ostheimer, J. *Achievement Motivation among the Chagga People of Tanzania.* East African Institute of Social Research Conference Report No. 343, 1965.

Owari, Thelma. "Changing Attitudes of Students in West African Society towards Marriage and Family Relationships." *British Journal of Sociology,* 1960, *11*, pp. 197-210.

Pettigrew, Thomas F., Allport, Gordon W., and Barnett, E. O. "Binocular Resolution and Perception of Race in South Africa." *British Journal of Psychology,* 1958 *49*, pp. 265-278.

60

Raum, Otto F. *Chagga Childhood: A Description of Indigenous Education in an East African Tribe.* London: Oxford University Press, 1940.

Read, Margaret. *Children of Their Fathers: Growing Up among the Ngoni of Nyasaland.* London: Methuen & Co. Ltd., 1959.

Ritchie, J. F. *The African as Suckling and as Adult (a Psychological Study).* Rhodes-Livingstone Institute, Paper No. 9, 1943.

————. "The African as Grown-Up Nursling." *Rhodes-Livingstone Journal,* 1944, *1,* pp. 55-60.

Segall, Marshall. *A Preliminary Report on Psychological Research in Ankole.* East African Institute of Social Research Conference Paper No. 116, 1959.

————. "Acquiescence and 'Identification with the Aggressor' among Acculturating Africans." *Journal of Social Psychology,* 1963, *61,* pp. 247-262.

Sherwood, E. T. "On the Designing of TAT Pictures with Special Reference to a Set for an African People Assimilating Western Culture." *Journal of Social Psychology,* 1957, *45,* pp. 161-190.

————. *Swazi Personality and the Assimilation of the Western Culture.* Unpublished doctoral dissertation, University of Chicago, 1961.

Somerset, H. C. A. *Home Structure, Parental Separation and Examination Success in Buganda.* East African Institute of Social Research Conference Paper No. 342, 1965.

Taylor, Andrew. *Educational Occupational Selection in West Africa.* London: Oxford University Press, 1962.

Uka, N. *Growing Up in Nigerian Culture.* Ibadan: Institute of Education, University College, Ibadan, Occasional Publication No. 6, 1966.

Valantin, S., and Collomb, H. "Étude Psychosociologique de la Situation Pédagogique au Sénégal." *Cahiers d'Études Africaines,* 1962, *11*(4), pp. 624-630.

Van der Post, Laurens. *The Heart of the Hunter.* London: Hogarth Press, 1961.

Verhaegen, Paul. "Utilité Actuelle des Tests pour l'Étude Psychologique des Autochtones Congolais." *Review de Psychologique Appliquée,* 1956, *6,* pp. 139-151.

————. "Study of the African Personality in the Belgian Congo." In Report of the C.S.A. Meeting of Specialists on the Basic Psychology of African and Madagascan Populations. *Scientific Council for Africa South of the Sahara,* Publication No. 51, 1959, Annex 11, pp. 1-9.

————. *L'Enfant Africain.* Paris: Bureau International de l'Enfance, Edition Fleurus, 1960.

————, and Laroche. "Some Methodological Considerations Concerning the Study of Aptitudes and the Elaboration of Psychological Tests for African Natives." *Journal of Social Psychology,* 1958, *47,* pp. 249-256.

————, and Leblanc, M. "Quelques Considérations au Sujet de l'Éducation Pré-Primaire de l'Enfant Noir." *Revue Pédagogique Congolais,* 1955, *2,* pp. 17-28.

Vincent, M. "L'Enfant au Ruanda-Urundi." *Mémoires de la Section des Sciences Naturelles et Médicoles de l'Institut Royal Colonial Belge,* 1954, *23.*

Wandira, A. R. *A Study of Indigenous and Western Education in Uganda (with Special Reference to Purpose and Practice).* Unpublished masters thesis, University of London, 1961.

Welbourn, Hebe. "Health Education for the Younger Child." *Journal of Tropical Medicine and Hygiene,* 1962.

————. "Customs and Child Health in Buganda. 2. Methods of Child Rearing." *Journal of Tropical and Geographical Medicine,* 1963, *15*, pp. 124-13̈3.

Whiting, Beatrice. *Six Cultures: Studies of Child Rearing.* New York: Wiley and Sons, 1963.

Whiting, John W. M. *Becoming a Kwoma.* New Haven: Yale University Press, 1941.

————, and Child, Irvin. *Child Training and Personality.* New Haven: Yale University Press, 1953.

V. Perceptual Cognition

An understanding of the world we live in and the development of our objective attitudes and mature responsibility depend upon a well-developed sense of spatial, temporal and causal relationships and these in turn depend on habits of visual as opposed to auditory synthesis.

Carothers, 1953, p. 103.

One of the greatest difficulties in interviewing Africans is the inability of many of them to report their own impressions, feelings and even actions. They may be willing to provide information but simply be unable to express themselves through lack of practice in situations resembling interviews.

Doob, 1961, p. 361.

The preceding chapter laid the foundation for discussing more specific areas of the African child's cognitive world. One aspect which has attracted the attention of many researchers is perceptual cognition. This chapter discusses three areas of specific research in that realm: (1) the susceptibility of different cross-cultural groups to perceptual illusions; (2) the use of two-dimensional materials to represent the world, more specifically, the use of the 7-Squares Test with Africans; and (3) the ability to interpret visual materials such as pictures and movies, and the difficulties encountered when these materials are used for educational purposes.

PERCEPTUAL ILLUSIONS

The susceptibility of different cultural groups to perceptual illusions has been the focus of several studies. Within Western cultures it has been found that when the viewer is presented with conflicting stimuli, he unconsciously applies his past experience and selects that which has the best predictive value for him. This may mean that the competing stimuli in the situation are irreconcilable and the viewer "sees" events which do not exist in reality. For example, if an individual in a dark room looks with one eye at two lines of light which are at an equal distance and elevation but of different lengths, the longer line will look nearer than the shorter line. Apparently, the observer assumes the lines are of equal length and translates the difference in length to a difference in position.

A technique which was developed to investigate complex perceptual situations is the "rotating trapezoidal window." It consists of a wooden frame in the shape of a trapezoid with six panes cut in the frame and shadows painted on it to give the appearance of a rectangular window. The frame is mounted so that it rotates slowly on its axis. A Western viewer at the distance of 25 feet does not interpret the figure as a rotating trapezoid, which it is, but as an oscillating rectangle; in other words, the observer's experience with rectangular windows influences his interpretation of the frame. In another experiment using the trapezoidal frame, a small cube is attached to the upper side of the short end of the frame. As the frame moves the cube appears to become detached, move freely around to the front of the frame, and attach itself once again.

In using this device with Africans, Gordon Allport and Thomas Pettigrew (1967) found that under "optimal illusion conditions" (at the distance of 25 feet, with the viewer using both eyes) there was no difference between African and European subjects in their susceptibility to the illusion; both groups interpreted the frame as a rectangle. However, under other conditions (such as binocular vision or at the distance of only ten feet) the Europeans still "see" the illusion, but rural Africans interpret the frame correctly as a trapezoid and do not see the small cube float free. The authors hypothesize that this is due to the rural African's lack of experience with rectangular windows and doors; they do not expect the frame to be rectangular. Urban Africans, on the other hand, have the same expectations as the Western viewer. The authors concluded that, as a result of his environment, the rural African is less sensitive to the directional properties of rectangular shapes.

M. B. Shapiro (1960) felt that his findings were contrary to those of Allport and Pettigrew. He compared Africans in Southern Rhodesia with brain damaged and mentally defective patients, as well as with normal Europeans. He found that in the rotation of the frame, Africans were influenced by the same directional features as Europeans, but to a greater degree. Shapiro attributed the African susceptibility to illusion to anxiety about the task they were asked to do, as well as unfamiliarity with the task and the culture they come from, which does not provide an opportunity for learning skills which would enable them to make an adequate integration of the directional properties of the visual world (p. 30).

Phyllis Morgan (1959b) hypothesized that there would be a difference in the perception of visual illusions among Zulus, Kalahari Bushmen, and white students in South Africa. After using a series of illusions with these groups, she found that results were not consistent from one test to another. On the Müller-Lyer Illusion the Zulus and Kalahari Bushmen were less affected than the Europeans, but on a Horizontal-Vertical Illusion they were more affected, and on a Perspective Illusion there was no significant difference between the three groups. Morgan felt that more research needed to be done on the influence of such factors as education and culture on the perception of illusion.

Marie Bonté (1960, 1962) hypothesized that Morgan's results might be attributed to the way the illusions are presented, and the different types of environment in which the tribes live. This she concluded from the results of the then current data from African tribes, as well as from two studies she did in the Congo. In her first study, Bonté used a set of fifteen Müller-Lyer Illusion figures with a group of Bambuti Pygmies in the North Kivu area of the Congo, with members of the Bashi tribe in Central Kivu province, and with Europeans. The pygmies are essentially gatherers and live in heavily forested areas. They are largely illiterate and it is hypothesized that they seldom see horizontal lines. The Bashi, in contrast, live on the shores of a lake, are agricultural people, and have frequent contact with Europeans.

With the first set of materials Bonté found it was not possible to test the Bambuti because they neither comprehended nor had the motivation necessary to concentrate on the task. On the other hand, although the Europeans were significantly more susceptible to the illusion than the Bashi, the magnitude of illusion was high for both groups. Bonté suggested that the high magnitude of susceptibility may have been the result of the order in which the figures were presented. The first eleven were in an ascending order of discrepancy and the last four were in reverse order. Subjects' responses to the first eleven figures provided them with a response set which may have continued through the last four figures. On a second experiment using Müller-Lyer figures, but presenting them through different materials, Bonté (1962) was able to test the Bambuti as well as the Bashi and Europeans. The results of this administration indicated no significant differences among the three cultural groups.

Using several illusion tests, Segall, Campbell, and Herskovits (1963) hypothesized that Africans living in urban areas are more likely to be affected by the Sanders-Parallelogram Illusion because of their experiences with an expectation of rectangularity. With the Horizontal-Vertical Illusion, the authors hypothesized, pastoral tribes would be more susceptible due to their habit of interpreting vertical images on the retina as lines extending horizontally into the distance (e.g., a furrow in a plowed field), for pastoral tribes live in flat, wide-open plains and have seen the horizon in this way many times. On the other hand, forest dwellers and those who live in crowded urban areas would more often interpret vertical images as vertical objects. Segall, Campbell, and Herskovits presented the illusions to twelve

African groups in different parts of Africa, as well as to South African whites, to Filipinos, and to two American samples. Their results showed a strong cultural difference in susceptibility to illusion, which supported their hypothesis that different perceptual habits develop as a result of different environments.

Clive Davis (1966) discussed the work of Segal, *et al.* (1963), and then hypothesized that selective attention may be a more important determinant of susceptibility to illusion than is environment. Davis, working in Uganda, did two sets of experiments to test this hypothesis. The first was basically a duplication of Segall's work among the Banyankole in Uganda. For the second set of experiments, Davis designed materials to specifically test the prediction that instructions to disregard or attend to specific features of the stimulus would affect the subject's performance on the tasks. Davis summarized his results by stating that instructions to ignore aspects of the stimulus which help create the illusion led to a decrease in susceptibility to the Müller-Lyer Illusion. He suggested that this finding offered support for the original hypothesis by Segall that the cross-cultural differences in the Müller-Lyer Illusion indicated in their study were not influenced by selective attention differences in the samples. Davis' work did not, however, duplicate the findings that there are significant cross-cultural differences in susceptibility to the Müller-Lyer Illusion.

Jahoda (1966) also set out to duplicate Segall's work. Working in Ghana, he selected subjects who varied both in terms of culture – Ghanaians and Britishers – and in terms of environment (the Ghanaian sample included people from tribes of contrasting environments similar to those Segall predicted would be more susceptible to illusions). Jahoda's sample included 213 Ghanaians and 43 Britishers. The results of his tests indicated significant over-all differences in the expected direction between the Ghanaians and the British subjects, but no significant differences in the susceptibility to illusions between the Ghanaian sub-groups.

TWO-DIMENSIONAL REPRESENTATIONS

Another aspect of perceptual cognition which has been studied is the African's ability to use two-dimensional representations to depict the world in which he lives. A series of studies was done using the 7-Squares Test with Africans in Mozambique and South Africa. The test itself consists of seven squares of different sizes which can be manipulated by the subject to make designs. In this test the subject manipulates two dimensions and may use these to represent three-dimensional objects.

Hector and Hudson (1959) presented this test to Portuguese East Africans and white South Africans. In looking at the designs produced by the subjects, they hypothesized that the "differences in mental endowment and educational attainment are responsible for differences in design" (p. 159). They also stated that the pattern created and preferred by the individual is a significant expression of his personality structure. The authors felt that this test is not culture-bound since "any type of design can be obtained from any candidate regardless of the cultural environment" (p. 160). The results of testing with the above groups indicated to the authors that the African had a "less stable" personality than the European.

Morgan (1959a) used the 7-Squares Test with literate and illiterate Africans in South Africa. The subjects were instructed to arrange the squares and then to title their pictures. Although judges were not able to recognize the designs of either group, the literate subjects were found to be more apt to make orderly designs than the illiterate, whose pictures showed less form. Morgan concluded that his work supported the hypothesis that there would be a difference in designs as a result of the educational achievement of the subjects (p. 47).

D. J. Bradley (1960) had a series of judges try to identify the subject in pictures which literate and illiterate Africans in South Africa had produced using the 7-Squares materials. From the fact that the judges were generally unable to identify the subject matter, Bradley concluded that black groups, "educated or illiterate, do not have the ability to structure recognizable representations . . . by means of the 7-Squares Test" (p. 144). It is important to note that this study had no control group.

One might hypothesize that the results of these studies may be more dependent on the imagination of the judges than on the work of the subjects. Also, it may be relevant to ask what kinds of experiences the subjects previously had with the objects they were asked to construct.

Hector, Dlodlo, and DuPlessis (1961) followed up the studies of Morgan and Bradley by presenting subjects with six pictures made from 7-Squares Test materials. Four pictures were representational, the other two were more abstract. The authors found that the ability to recognize representative silhouettes improves with age. They also found that a child's readiness to name nonrepresentative silhouettes decreases with age (p. 198).

Some of the above researchers used the 7-Squares Test as a test of the subject's ability to create a picture of his three-dimensional world by using two dimensions. At the same time other investigators were working on the interpretation of existing pictures in an attempt to explore the African's ability to read pictures rather than to construct them. Initial work in this area was done through exploration of the difficulties many Africans had in interpreting depth in pictures.

Hudson (1960) was one of the first individuals to do research into the African child's ability to perceive depth in pictures. He suggested that in providing an educational system for Africans, and in creating books and other materials used in the schools, many assumptions were being made about the child's ability, some of which he felt were not valid and should be questioned. From his experiments with African children, Hudson formulated the following hypotheses: (1) In a cultural group of normal intellectual endowment which is closely associated with the dominant cultural norm, pictorial depth perception is dependent upon both intellectual and educational thresholds. As the educational level rises, the intellectual threshold ceases to be critical. (2) In a cultural group below average in intelligence and isolated from the cultural norm, pictorial depth perception is independent of educational level. The intelligence and cultural thresholds are critical. (3) In a cultural group which has a normal intelligence range, but which lives in isolation from the dominant cultural norm, pictorial depth perception is independent of both the educational and intellectual level. The cultural threshold is critical. (4) In a cultural group which has a normal intelligence range and possesses high educational qualifications, but which is isolated from the dominant cultural norm, pictorial depth perception is not closely related to intellectual endowment or to educational achievement. The cultural threshold is critical. (1962b). These hypotheses led Hudson to conclude that there is a need to adapt educational methods to prevailing conditions. He called for a scientific turn of mind in the teaching of African children, a healthy skepticism about existing educational procedures, and a deliberate emphasis on psychological research to study the African child (1962b).

Jan Deregowski (1966a), somewhat skeptical of Hudson's conclusions about Africans' depth perception, did an experiment employing two methods to test perceptual skills. The first was the test devised by Hudson, the second a situation in which students constructed models from pictures. Deregowski found that on Hudson's test African subjects had difficulty interpreting depth perception, but when the subjects constructed models from pictures they were three-dimensional, as were the objects depicted in the pictures. This indicated that the subjects were able to interpret depth in a two-dimensional representation. Deregowski concluded that the ability to interpret depth in a test situation depends on the type of response required and the nature of the drawings used.

INTERPRETING VISUAL MATERIALS

A series of studies has been done on the use of films in African communities. As a result of their works, several authors suggest that it is very difficult to predict how people will react to the material presented in a film. Dickson (1945) reported the amazement of a group of Africans when they saw a newsreel which presented a known dignitary. In one scene he was reviewing an honor guard and was in military dress. In the subsequent scene he was seen in evening dress in a reception line for visiting dignitaries. The audience was confused by the quick change of dress and the compression of time. Bever (1952) found that audiences frequently focused on one aspect and failed to understand the total picture. His subjects were also confused by scanning procedures. The fast movement of the camera was interpreted as houses moving which increased and decreased in size.

Morton-Williams (1953), experimenting to find the most effective use of films, presented 34 films in four different parts of Nigeria. He found that color did not increase enjoyment or interest for the audience. Some of the subjects even failed to realize the film was in color. Morton-Williams also found that audiences would frequently become very involved in the action of the film and participate both actively and vocally as the film proceeded (p. 50). The author felt that it is difficult to know what the individual has perceived, since frequently people would focus their attention on parts of the film which were irrelevant to the purposes of the producer. Thus, those who are writing and producing films for use in Africa – particularly films for educational purposes – must have a sophisticated knowledge about their potential audience.

Doob (1961) did a picture interpretation study with educated and uneducated adults in a Fulani community in Northern Nigeria. With these subjects he used both drawings and photographs. The subjects in this experiment were not baffled by the task of identifying the photographs or drawings. However, they did have trouble discussing the pictures. They would point out specific individuals or objects in the pictures, but failed to relate these to the picture as a whole. Doob suggested that the critical factor in the subjects' identification may not have been familiarity with the content, but rather lack of familiarity with the technique of presentation (p. 273). Doob then presented the pictures in different ways. He informed one set of subjects that they would be asked to recall the pictures later. This technique did not help the subject to discuss the pictures better. A second technique was to ask the subjects to show the investigator a specific item in the picture. This the subjects could do. Doob concluded from this that:

> Africans at this level of education and contact with Western media either perceive more than they report or else easily can be made to perceive more when they are requested to do so. If anything they suffer from a lack of experience with drawings and photographs but this difficulty can be quickly overcome. Without doubt they do not readily express what they perceive (p. 275).

Bantu workers' ability to interpret a set of safety posters was analyzed by Wendy Winter (1963), who presented a series of them to men in industry for a discussion with them. In her article she included pictures of the posters used, and described the aspects of each poster which were misleading. The article is interesting in that it shows how important learning is in the perception of pictures. Winter also included recommendations for drawing pictures. These recommendations emphasize the importance of depicting scenes in accordance with the prevailing cultural tradition, both in terms of behavior and the symbolic meanings of objects, shapes, and colors.

Winter's work suggests that the African's reactions may be a result of his culturally characteristic ways of perceiving, rather than an "error" in perception. This same idea was proposed as early as 1933 by R. H. Thouless, whose work suggested that the way people perceive pictures is dependent on the culture in which they live. Nadel's (1937) analysis of the Nupe and Yoruba in Nigeria also indicated that culture has a strong effect on what is perceived. A further example of cultural influences on perception is offered by Littlejohn (1963), who postulated that the Bantu's use of space – which differs markedly from that of the European – might be responsible for difficulties in depth perception. More recently DuToit (1966) has hypothesized that trouble with depth perception is due to the different linguistic structures of languages.

Many authors feel that the main influence on the child's ability to comprehend and learn from pictorial material is adequate exposure to appropriate experiences. Alan Holmes (1963) felt that work done cross-culturally on perception confirmed the assumption that the ability to interpret pictorial symbols is a learned skill, and in that sense has much in common with the ability to interpret verbal presentations. The experiences Arthur French (1963) had in East Africa led him to conclude that perception is a learned phenomenon which had not yet been investigated. French presented a series of pictures of Kenya to students in Uganda. While the students did not have direct experience with the content of the pictures, they had closely associated experiences. He found that students had difficulty in interpretation, in gaining perspective, and in reacting correctly to differences in light and shade in photographs and pictures. French concluded that the poverty of the environment is a sufficient explanation for these perceptual difficulties, and his work indicated that the use of pictures as concrete representations of abstract ideas may not be helpful in developing concepts, since pictures are not correctly interpreted.

To what extent can this difficulty be overcome? Results of the visual perception tests used by MacArthur, *et al.* (1964) as part of their mental abilities survey showed that "visual perception weakness, commonly associated with Africans, may be remedied through appropriate educational techniques" (p. 3). McFie (1961) concluded from his experiment on the effects of education on student's performance on intelligence tests that "an ability which may be poorly developed under [existing] cultural conditions, and which may be increased by appropriate educational methods, is that of perceiving visual materials as a whole" (p. 232). In a later article, French (1966) discussed the fact that earlier hopes of analyzing the skills of perception and devising ways of teaching them were naive. Perception is complex. It is a subtle pheonmenon influenced by previous experience and made up of complex psychological as well as optical components. More must be understood about the total process before it can be understood how perceptual skills are influenced by differing environments.

BIBLIOGRAPHY

Allport, Gordon, and Pettigrew, Thomas. "Cultural Influence on the Perception of Movement: The Trapezoidal Illusion among Zulus." *Journal of Abnormal and Social Psychology,* 1957, *55,* pp. 104-114.

Bever, L. "The Cinema as a Means of Education in the Belgian Congo." In *Visual Aids in Fundamental Education.* Paris: UNESCO, 1952, pp. 59-67.

Beveridge, W. M. "Radial Differences in Phenomenal Regression." *British Journal of Psychology,* 1935, *26,* pp. 59-62.

———. "Some Racial Differences in Perception." *British Journal of Psychology,* 1939, *30*(1), pp. 57-64.

Bonté, Marie. *Contribution à l'Étude des Illusions Optico-Géometriques.* Unpublished doctoral dissertation, Université Catholique de Louvain, 1960.

———. "The Reaction of Two African Societies to the Müller-Lyer Illusion." *Journal of Social Psychology,* 1962, *58,* pp. 265-268.

Bradley, D. J. "The Ability of Black Groups to Produce Recognizable Patterns on the 7-Squares Test." *Journal of the National Institute of Personnel Relations,* 1960, *8,* pp. 142-144.

———. "Problems of Recognition in Bantu Testing." *Perceptual and Motor Skills,* 1964, *19,* p. 718ff.

Cowley, J. J., and Murray, M. "Some Aspects of the Development of Spatial Concepts in Zulu Children." *Journal of Social Research,* 1962, *13,* pp. 1-18.

Davis, Clive. *The Strength of the Müller-Lyer Illusion as a Function of Attentional Factors.* Proceedings of the East Africa Social Science Conference, Kampala, Uganda, December 1966.

Dennis, W. "Cultural and Development Factors in Perception." In R. R. Blake and G. V. Ramsey (eds.). *Perception, An Approach to Personality.* New York: Ronald Press Co., 1951, pp. 148-169.

Deregowski, Jan. *Difficulties in Pictorial Perception in Africa.* Human Development Research Unit, Institute of Social Research, University of Zambia, 1966a, No. 1.

———. *Influence of Perspective upon Perception of Pictorially Represented Volume in Bantu Schoolboys.* Human Development Research Unit, Institute of Social Research, University of Zambia, 1966b, No. 3.

———. "Investigation into Perception." *Bulletin of the Institute of Social Research,* University of Zambia, 1966c, *1,* pp. 27-30.

———. *The Horizontal-Vertical Illusion and the Ecological Hypothesis.* Human Research Development Unit, Institute of Social Research, University of Zambia, 1967, No. 4.

———. "Pictorial Recognition in Subjects from a Relatively Pictureless Environment." *African Social Research,* 1969.

72

Dickson, A. C. "Studies in War-Time Organization: III. The Mobile Propaganda Unit, East Africa Command." *African Affairs*, 1945, *44*, pp. 9-18.

Doob, Leonard. *Communication in Africa: A Search for Boundaries.* New Haven: Yale University Press, 1961.

————. "Eidetic Imagery among the Ibo." *Ethnology*, 1964, *3*, pp. 357-363.

————. "Exploring Eidetic Imagery among the Kamba of Central Kenya." *Journal of Social Psychology*, 1965a, *67*, pp. 3-22.

————. "Psychology" In R. A. Lystad (ed.). *The African World: A Survey of Social Research.* London: Pall Mall Press, 1965b, pp. 373-415 and 543-549.

————. "Eidetic Imagery: A Cross-Cultural Will-o'-the Wisp? " *Journal of Psychology*, 1966, *63*, pp. 13-34.

DuToit, B. M. "Pictorial Depth Perception and Linguistic Relativity." *Psychologica Africana*, 1966, *11*, pp. 51-63.

Fabian, H. "An Experiment with Two Forms of the 7-Squares Test." *Journal of the National Institute of Personnel Research*, 1959, *8*, pp. 56-58.

Falmange, J. "Étude Comparative de Développement Psychomoteur: Classe des Sciences Naturelles et Médicales." *Memoires*, 1962, *13*(5).

Film Centre, London. "The Use of Mobile Cinema and Radio Vans." In *Visual Aids in Fundamental Education.* Paris: UNESCO, 1949.

Fortes, Meyer. *Social and Psychological Aspects of Education in Taleland.* London: Oxford University Press, for the International Institute of African Languages and Cultures, 1938.

French, Arthur. "A Background of Non-Reference." *Makerere Journal*, 1961, *5*.

————. "Methods and Media and Some Differences in Visual Communication." *Journal of Tropical Medicine and Hygiene*, 1962.

————. "The Comprehension of Pictures." *Visual Education*, 1963.

————. "The Perception of Pictures. In *Report of the Seminar on the Perception of Pictures and Its Relation to Education.* Makerere University College, Kampala, Uganda, 1966.

Hall, D. *How Africans See Pictures.* Syracuse, New York: New Readers Press, 1962.

Harmon, R. J. "An Experiment in Testing Aural Perception in English with a Group of Shona Speaking African Children of Different Ages." *Rhodes-Livingstone Journal*, 1963, *34*, pp. 36-43.

Harris, Verona. "Colour Perception and Language." In *Report of the Seminar on the Perception of Pictures and Its Relation to Education.* Makerere University College, Kampala, Uganda, 1966.

Haward, L. C. R., and Roland, W. A. "Some Intercultural Differences on the Draw-A-Man Test: I. Goodenough Score." *Man*, 1954, *54*, pp. 86-88.

————. "Some Intercultural Differences on the Draw-A-Man Test: II. Machover Series." *Man*, 1955a, *55*, pp. 27-29.

————. "Some Intercultural Differences on the Draw-A-Man Test: III. Conclusion." *Man*, 1955b, *55*, pp. 40-42.

Hector, H., Dlodlo, D. S., and DuPlessis, C. F. "An Experiment in Silhouette Recognition and Projection with Bantu Children of Different Ages. *Journal of the National Institute of Personnel Research*, 1961, *8*, pp. 195-198.

Hector, H., and Hudson, W. "Pattern Specificity in a Sample of Mozambique Tribesmen on the 7-Squares Test." *Journal of the National Institute of Personnel Research,* 1959, *7,* pp. 156-161.

Heuse, G. A. "Études Psychologiques surs les Noirs Sudannais et Guinéens." *Revue de Psychologie des Peuples,* 1957, *12,* pp. 35-68.

Holmes, Alan. *A Study of Understanding Visual Symbols in Kenya.* London: OVAC, 1963.

Hudson, W. "Pictorial Depth Perception in Subcultural Groups in Africa." *Journal of Social Psychology,* 1960, *52,* pp. 183-208.

―――――. "Cultural Problems in Pictorial Perception." *South African Journal of Science,* 1962a, *58* (7), pp. 189-195.

―――――. "Pictorial Perception and Educational Adaptation in Africa." *Psychologica Africana,* 1962b, *9,* pp. 226-239.

―――――. *Pictorial Depth Perception Test.* National Institute of Personnel Research, South African Council for Scientific and Industrial Research, no date.

"Information and Cinema in Africa South of the Sahara." *Monthly Bulletin,* 1958, *9,* pp. 1-5.

Izod, A. "Fundamental Education by Film in Central Africa." In *Visual Aids in Fundamental Education.* Paris: UNESCO, 1952.

Jahoda, Gustav. "Geometric Illusions and Environment: A Study in Ghana." *British Journal of Psychology,* 1966, *57,* pp. 193-199.

Kingdom, Jonathan. *The Effective Use of Pictorial Material.* Makerere University College, Kampala, Uganda, 1966.

Larken. "Impressions of the Azande." *Sudan Notes and Records,* 1926, *9,* pp. 1-55 and 1927, *10,* pp. 85-134.

Laroche, J. L. "L'Analyse des Erreurs sur le Matrix 38." *Bulletin Centrale d'Et, et Recherche Psychotechnique,* 1956, *5,* pp. 161-172.

Littlejohn, J. "Temne Space." *Anthropological Quarterly,* 1963, *63,* pp. 1-17.

Lystad, Mary. "Paintings of Ghanaian Children." *Africa,* 1960, *30,* pp. 238-242.

MacArthur, Robert, Irvine, Sidney, and Brimble, Arthur. *The Northern Rhodesia Mental Ability Survey, 1963.* Lusaka: Rhodes-Livingstone Institute, 1964.

McFie, John. "The Effects of Education on African Performance on a Group of Intellectual Tests." *British Journal of Educational Psychology,* 1961, *31,* pp. 232-240.

Morgan, Phyllis. "A Study of Perceptual Differences among Cultural Groups in Southern Africa Using Tests of Geometric Illusion." *Journal of the National Institute of Personnel Research,* 1959a, *8,* pp. 39-43.

―――――. "Observations and Findings on the 7-Squares Test with Literate and Illiterate Black Groups in Southern Africa." *Journal of the National Institute of Personnel Research,* 1959b, *8,* pp. 44-47.

Morton-Williams. *Cinema in Rural Nigeria.* Zaria: Federal Information Service, 1953.

Mundy-Castle, A. C. *Pictorial Depth Perception in Ghanaian Children,* 1966.

Nadel, S. F. "A Field Experiment in Racial Psychology." *British Journal of Psychology,* 1937, *28,* pp. 195-211.

N.H.D.S. "A Theory Regarding Mental Reaction to the Sound of Native Proper Names." *NADA* (Salisbury, the Southern Rhodesian Native Affairs Department Annual), 1934, *12*, pp. 79-81.

Nissen, H. W., *et al.* "A Study of Performance Tests Given to a Group of Native African Negro Children." *British Journal of Psychology*, 1935, *25* (3), pp. 308-355.

Ombredane, André, Bertelson, Paul, and Beniest-Noirot, Elaine. "Speed and Accuracy of Performance of an African Native Population and of Belgian Children on a Paper and Pencil Perceptual Test." *Journal of Social Psychology*, 1958, *47*, pp. 327-337.

Pettigrew, Thomas, Allport, Gordon, and Barnett, E. "Binocular Resolution and Perception of Race in South Africa." *British Journal of Psychology*, 1958, *49* (4), pp. 265-278.

Pratt, C. A. "A Code for the Use of Illustrations of Educational Material for Use in Primary Schools in East Africa." In *Report of the Seminar on the Perception of Pictures and Its Relation to Education.* Makerere University College, Kampala, Uganda, 1966, pp. 8-11.

Schwitzgebel, R. "The Performance of Dutch and Zulu Adults on Selected Perceptual Tasks." *Journal of Social Psychology*, 1962, *57*, pp. 73-77.

Segall, Marshall, Campbell, Donald, and Herskovits, Melville. "Cultural Differences in the Perception of Geometrical Illusions." *Science*, 1963, *139* (3556), pp. 769-771.

―――. *The Influence of Culture on Perception.* New York: Bobbs-Merrill, 1966.

Shapiro, M. B. "The Rotation of Drawings by Illiterate Africans." *Journal of Social Psychology*, 1960, *52*, pp. 17-30.

―――. *The Influence of Social Environment on the Rotation of Drawings.* Unpublished manuscript, 1961.

Sherwood, E. T. "On the Designing of TAT Pictures with Specific References to a Set for an African People Assimilating Western Culture." *Journal of Social Psychology*, 1957, *45*, pp. 161-190.

Simon, K. "Colour Vision of the Buganda." *East African Medical Journal*, 1951, *28*, pp. 75-79.

Suchman, Rosslyn. "Cultural Differences in Children's Color and Form Perception." *Journal of Social Psychology*, 1966, *70*, pp. 3-10.

Taylor, G. A. "Primitive Color Vision." *NADA*, 1934, *12*, pp. 64-67.

Thouless, R. H. "A Racial Difference in Perception." *Journal of Social Psychology*, 1933, *4*, pp. 330-339.

Wingard, P. G. "Educational Research in Countries Other than the U.S.: East Africa." *Review of Educational Research*, 1962, *32*, pp. 293-295.

Winter, Wendy. "The Perception of Safety Posters by Bantu Industrial Workers." *Psychologica Africana*, 1963, *10*, pp. 127-135.

Wolofsky, A., and Carroll, B. J. *A Comparative Study in Rotation of Gestalt Designs.* Nairobi, Kenya: Ministry of Education, 1964.

VI. Cognitive Development

It would seem from... investigations that the South African native has not the learning ability to be able to compete on equal terms with the average European, except in tasks of an extremely simple nature.

Van Rensenburg, 1933, p. 43.

We begin with the hypothesis that any subject can be taught effectively in some intellectually honest form to any child at any stage of development.... The task of teaching a subject to a child at any particular age is one of representing the structure of that subject in terms of the child's way of viewing things.

Bruner, 1962, p. 33.

Reference has been made to studies of the general intelligence of the African in Chapter II, and Chapter V includes references on one aspect of cognition − perceptual cognition. In this chapter the work of researchers who have attempted to assess other specific cognitive skills is reviewed.

ABSTRACT THINKING

Many of the early philosophical works, such as Lévy-Bruhl's (1926), suggested that the African lives in a world of concrete objects and is unable to do abstract thinking. Similar statements were made by other authors such as Carothers (1953) and Haward and Roland (1955). Jahoda (1956) maintained that these authors did not have adequate ways of assessing the abstract abilities of non-Western peoples, since Western tests of abstract behavior cannot be validly applied in non-Western societies. These tests are no more culture free than are tests of intelligence (p. 242). In his own work, Jahoda found that the ability to do abstract thinking is strongly affected by the environment of the child. He felt that the environment was crucial for developing abstracting skills, and it is the lack of these skills which has led investigators using tests dependent on them to conclude that abstracting ability is absent. Jahoda also pointed out that there are abstract thinking skills which are developed traditionally; this is illustrated, for example, by the abilities required to play the game "Owari."

Price-Williams (1962) took the same position as Jahoda on the use of Western tests in Africa. In reviewing past investigations of the cognitive processes of primitive peoples, he noted that researchers reached conclusions about the inability of Africans to use abstract thinking, although they used Western tests in a non-Western setting. He felt that previous investigators had not made valid assumptions about the ability of their subjects. In his experiments with the Tiv in Nigeria, Price-Williams (1961a, b) used materials and techniques based on the Tiv culture. He emphasized the importance of using local materials, rather than foreign objects which would confound perceptual skills. Price-Williams accompanied his experiments with a description of the Tiv tribe in relation to the social structure and language features which might have an effect on test results. He noted that the Tiv culture contains fairly complex abstract systems in such social categories as kinship, marriage, property, and laws. However, in relation to objects, the concrete is more dominant.

In one experiment Price-Williams (1961a) gave children a compound series test. This required the concentration of the child on an intellectual task. A series of beads was presented to the child who was told to add the next beads in the series. The results showed that shape was given greater emphasis than was the color of the beads. In this test, color was the least important visual cue.

In another experiment (1961b) children in rural Tiv communities, schooled and unschooled, were instructed to sort and classify models of animals and plants found in the region. Price-Williams asked the children why they had sorted the objects in the manner they did, and recorded the degree of abstraction evident in their reasons. The children showed a progression of stages of equivalence grouping as Piaget has described, although they attained these stages at a later age than did their European counterparts. There was no significant difference between the literate and the illiterate children in terms of whether they progressed from color to form to function in equivalence grouping. Price-Williams attributed this to the use of objects equally familiar to all the children, thus eliminating the advantages which might have occurred through school learning (1962, p. 60). He also noted that the abstractions present in grouping were not fully determined by the existing language classification. For example, domesticity of animals was an understood category although there is no term to describe it in the Tiv language.

Other experiments related to African children's equivalence grouping have been carried out by Rosslyn Suchman (1966), Robert Serpell (1966) and Patricia Greenfield (1966a, b). Research done with children in Western cultures shows that as children grow older they move from a preference for color to a preference for form. They then gain a concept of function and move to more abstract reasons for grouping. These preference changes are viewed as a correlate of cognitive growth.

In an attempt to test the universality of this theory, and to understand more about the thinking processes of African children, Suchman gave three color versus form tests to children in Nigeria between the ages of three and fifteen. The results indicated that age is not a variable in a preference for form, since all ages clearly chose color over form. (p. 7). These results suggested three things to Suchman: (1) In terms of developmental theory, the concept of a universal maturational process in perceptual color-form preference must be modified, if not abandoned. Maturation alone is not sufficient to change the preference from color to form. (2) Color preference may be more functional in certain cultures and more rewarding than form preference. In Western schools attention to form is reinforced. (3) This experiment provides an indication of the thinking processes in another culture, and hopefully will lead to a better understanding of the cultural differences in cognitive processes.

Serpell did an experiment in Zambia with Primary II children and illiterate counterparts matched in age, sex, and socio-economic levels. He was attempting to see if literate and illiterate children were significantly different in their use of form and color for grouping objects. Serpell found no significant difference between the schooled and unschooled group in the proportion of form and color responses made. The responses did indicate that the greater the difference between the colors of the choice objects, the greater the chance of response matching by color. Also, the more familiar – or readily named – the shapes, the more likely it was that children would use shape for matching (p. 39). Thus, it would appear that stimulus objects play an important part in determining children's performance on sorting tasks. Serpell also found that in the earliest school-age levels the two groups showed no significant difference in their choices. He is presently exploring the possibility that with more schooling there may be a difference in response patterns.

In experiments on equivalence carried out with Wolof children in Senegal, Greenfield, Reich, and Olver found that schooling was a significant factor in the children's use of color, form, and function. Among their findings were: Bush children who do not go to school are influenced by color at every stage of development. School children, in contrast, move away from an initial reliance on color. Bush children who go to school move mainly toward form, while city chilren who go to school move toward form and function. Thus, school appears to favor the growth of perceptual equivalence based on form (p. 315). When they discovered this emphasis on color groupings by unschooled bush children, they added a group of illiterate adults to their sample to find out if color grouping is persistent into adulthood. The only difference between the children and adults was that the adults were more consistent in their color groupings. The use of color becomes "improved" in the sense that the adult is able to make finer perceptual discriminations based on color. The authors suggested that this may be interpreted as an increase in intellectual rigidity and indicates a decrease in group variability (p. 296).

As noted above, Price-Williams found that schooling was not a significant variable in whether children were grouped on the basis of function (1961b). Greenfield, Reich, and Olver suggested that this may be due to the objects used by Price-Williams, which used in the appropriate context, whereas the experiments in Senegal utilized arbitrary contexts. Perhaps it is easier to see functional differences for the same type of items than it is to discover functional similarities among an isolated group of things (p. 297).

LANGUAGE AND COGNITIVE DEVELOPMENT

In their articles, each of the above authors made reference to the effects of language on the concept formation of children. The relationship between language and culture has been much debated. No attempt has been made in this review to include all the relevant sources on this subject. However, a few articles are included here which suggest the relationship between language and the cognitive development of the child within different cultures.

As early as 1935, Benjamin Whorf was developing a theory of linguistic relativity. Language, as viewed by Whorf, is a system of categories which expresses the world view of a culture and acts to perpetuate that culture. Certain aspects of different cultures are expressed in more linguistic detail than others. Whorf suggested that the structure of the language determines the type of thinking that individuals within the society can use.

Roger Brown (1956) maintained that rather than there being a difference in the concepts possible within a culture, there is a difference in the "availability" of the concepts in question (p. 307). This degree of availability, or frequency of occurrence, is determined by the needs of the society for the concept. Experiences are more easily coded in some societies because they occur more often, both verbally and cognitively. Brown defined language as "nothing less than an inventory of all the ideas, interests, and occupations that take up the attention of the community" (p. 311). Thus, a study of language may well give insights into the values and ways of thinking of a society.

The experiments by Price-Williams, Suchman, Serpell, and Greenfield illustrate the fact that the absence of a word to express a concept does not necessarily mean that individuals in the society are unable to use the concept. For example, Price-Williams noted that although a word for domestic animals is not present in the Tiv language the children utilized the concept in their equivalence groupings (1962). Greenfield, Reich, and Olver (1966) found that Wolof children have very few color words, "yet this fact does not stop monolingual Wolof children from relying almost exclusively upon color words in the formation of equivalence groupings" (p. 301).

A study done specifically on the effect of language on color perception was completed by Verona Harris (1966). She noted that the word "red" in the Zulu language is used to denote all colors from dark brown through yellow. She then asked the question: Does this indicate that the Zulus are deficient in color discrimination? For her sample she used rural and urban Zulus and matched them with a white sample. She then showed them color cards. Although the Zulus initially called all the cards "red," when questioned further they discriminated the colors through association (e.g., this is the color of my father's hut, this is the color of my uncle's largest cow). Although words for these colors are not present in children's vocabulary, "the Zulu children showed a finer discriminatory ability from brown to yellow and black to white than did the control groups of white children" (p. 12). The blue-green series was discriminated equally well by both groups. Harris concluded that the classification of color is made according to cultural demands and are accurate as long as they relate to cultural needs.

SPATIAL DEVELOPMENT

Another aspect of cognitive development is spatial development. The growth of spatial concepts in Zulu children was explored by Cowley and Murray (1962), who administered a series of tests of spatial development, devised by Piaget and Inhelder, to Zulu and white children ranging in age from five to twelve. Ten children were tested at each age level. Results showed that the white children closely followed the pattern of development of the children studied by Piaget and Inhelder, while the Zulu children showed the same stages of development, but at a later age.

Cowley and Murray suggested that in order to understand the factors influencing cognitive processes, it is necessary to isolate features of the culture which may play a part in cognitive development. They hypothesized that by understanding the general developmental level of the culture, one will be able to understand the cognitive level of groups within the culture. The authors concluded that when researchers look at a child's schooling, his familiarity with test materials and procedures, and the dimensions of his home environment, they are ignoring what determines these dimensions. They suggested that emphasis should be placed on studying the total culture in terms of the cognitive processes developed *within* the culture if there is to be meaningful understanding of what facilitates and limits intellectual development.

The development of time concepts in Ibo children in Nigeria was analyzed by N. Uka (1962), who designed a test, based on what he knew of the Ibo society, to look at the sequence of acquisition of time concepts, the age at which they are adequately developed, and the variations that occur within age, social status, and sex groups. For his test he chose 202 students between six and thirteen. Results showed that the boys obtained time concepts significantly earlier than did the girls. Uka attributed this to the fact that the boys are more socially mobile and are encouraged to be more vocal than girls. Uka's article contains a list of factors he felt influenced the development of time concepts. He then recommended that a greater emphasis be placed on an organized presentation of time concepts within the first year of school, since many school activities involve these concepts.

Shirley Hill (1964) worked with Ghanaian and American first-grade children to look at the way they developed mathematical concepts. The two concepts the children were tested on were identity of sets and identity of ordered sets. Results showed that identity of sets is an easily learned concept for both American and Ghanaian first-graders. A trend in the data indicated that initially American children responded correctly to ordered sets, while Ghanaian children responded correctly to identical sets. Hill hypothesized that each culture has produced a "natural" or preferred concept (p. 222), and that knowing the preferred concept of a cultural group is important in the designing of relevant educational experiences. In her analysis, Hill steered away from quantitative cross-cultural comparisons, considering them invalid due to the composition of the sample. The Ghanaian children were more heterogeneous than their American counterparts who all came from high-income families. Also, the children in America had a full year of kindergarten before first grade, and were more familiar with the tasks. English was used as the language medium with the Ghanaian children; this is a second language for them. Hill's article contains a full description of the tests used and a statistical analysis of the results.

Basil Chaplin (1963a, b, c) did a series of experiments in 1956 and 1960 with school children in Ghana. His findings showed that Ghanaian children are in no way different from their British and American counterparts in their understanding of natural phenomena. Also, the kind of educational background the Ghanaian child has does not affect his ability to comprehend natural phenomena. Chaplin also concluded that all children are capable of understanding some scientific process provided: (1) they are given personal experience at every stage of the process, and (2) the various stages are presented in their logical order (1963c, pp. 147-148).

While Ghanaian children seem to have no difficulty understanding and explaining the results of their own practical experiments, they have some difficulty with experiments outside their realm of experience. Older children seemed to be more handicapped than those between the ages of seven and eleven. This is due to the difference in the richness of and physical experience with the environment, which the younger children currently enjoy, but which was not generally available to the older ones when they were young. It is further aggravated by an educational system which emphasizes rote learning rather than developing critical thinking skills (1963b, p. 6).

CONCEPT OF CONSERVATION

Greenfield, (1966b) some of whose work was described earlier, also did a study of children's conservation concepts. She described her work as a study of the intellectual development in a society where the culturally given "technologies" are different from those found in the West (p. 226). By using Piaget's experiments involving the conservation of liquids, Greenfield asked the question: Are there differences in cognitive functioning cross-culturally? The answer being yes, she attempted to analyze those found. Her sample included nine groups, composed of three age groups (six-seven, eight-nine, eleven-thirteen) in each of three settings (rural unschooled, rural schooled, urban schooled). Her results showed no significant difference between the performance of nine- and thirteen-year olds in the unschooled group. She also found that intellectual development − defined as any qualitative change − does not occur after the age of nine without school experience (p. 234). The schooled children, both rural and urban, showed the same pattern of development as those in the West. Greenfield's results suggest that experience is indeed important in the development of the concept of conservation.

Greenfield also looked at the children's reasoning in the conservation experiments. Her analysis of the responses led her to conclude that there is a wider gap in understanding between the schooled and unschooled than between the rural and urban child. There are also factors within the Wolof language which affect the way children reach conservation. American children reach it through a period of conflict between appearance and reality, with reality finally coming to the fore-front. However, in Wolof, there is no way to express a reality-appearance conflict − Senegalese do not distinguish between the two. Thus, Senegalese children reach conservation through seeing the continuity of the past and the present.

These experiments led Greenfield to the hypothesis that different modes of thought can lead to the same results:

> It has too often been assumed that different means must of necessity lead to different cognitive ends. This might occur in the case of problems which have no objectivity definable "right" answer. But where there are action constraints and consequences of behavior (as with the phenomena of conservation) a disparity in result is not necessarily the case (1966b, p. 255).

In reviewing the works included in this chapter it is possible to see that experimental studies into the cognitive processes of the African peoples are a recent occurrence, few studies being done before 1960. Currently, there is a growing interest in this field, since it provides information about the universality of existing theories in educational psychology, and also provides a valuable understanding of the child's background and abilities when he enters the school situation. In the concluding chapter, which presents a review of current research, there are a number of references to work in the field of cognitive development within African cultures.

BIBLIOGRAPHY

Abiola, E. T. "The Nature of Intellectual Development in Nigerian Children." *Teacher Education,* 1965, *6*, pp. 37-58.

Biesheuvel, Simon. "Some African Acculturation Problems with Special Reference to Perceptual and Psychomotor Skills." *Symposium: The Interrelation of Biological and Cultural Adaptation.* Wenner-Gren Foundation, 1966.

Bohanon, Paul. "Concepts of Time among the Tiv of Nigeria." *Southwestern Journal of Anthropology,* 1953, *9*, pp. 251-262.

Brewster, P. G. "Some Nigerian Games with Their Parallels and Analogies." *Journal de la Société des Africanistes,* 1954, *24*, pp. 25-48.

Brown, Roger. "Language and Categories." In J. S. Bruner, *et al., A Study of Thinking.* New York: John Wiley & Sons, Inc., 1956, pp. 247-312.

Bruner, Jerome S. *The Process of Education.* Cambridge: Harvard University Press, 1962.

Carothers, J. C. *The African Mind in Health and Disease.* Geneva: WHO, 1953.

Carroll, J. B., and Casagrande, J. B. "The Function of Language Classifications on Behavior." In Maccoby, Newcomb, and Hartley (eds.). *Readings in Social Psychology.* New York: Holt, Rinehart & Co., 1958.

Chaplin, Basil. *The Development of African Elementary Science Education.* University of Ghana, 1963a.

―――――. *Notes on the Present Elementary Science (USA) Study in Relation to Science Study in West Africa.* University of Ghana, 1963b.

―――――. "Science Education in Ghana." *Overseas Education,* 1963c, *34.*

Clignet, Rémi. "Réflexions sur les Problèmes de Psychologie en Afrique." *Bulletin de l'Institut National d'Étude du Travail et d'Orientation Professionnelle,* 1962, *18.*

Cowley, J. J., and Murray, M. "Some Aspects of the Development of Spatial Concepts in Zulu Children." *Journal of Social Research,* 1962, *13*, pp. 1-18.

Dawson, J. L. *Psychological Effects of Social Change in a West Africa Community.* Unpublished doctoral dissertation, University of Edinburgh, 1963.

Doob, Leonard. "The Effect of Language on Verbal Expression and Recall." *American Anthropologist,* 1957, *59*, pp. 88-100.

English, D. R. "The Difficulties Experienced by the African Child in Learning Physics." *Journal of Education of New Africa,* 1964, *1* (11), pp. 12-15.

Etuk, E. *"The Development of Number Concepts: An Examination of Piaget's Theory with Yoruba Speaking Nigerian Children.* Unpublished doctoral dissertation, Columbia University, 1967.

Fortes, Meyer. "The Learning Ability of the South African Native." *Africa,* 1939, *12*, pp. 484-485.

Greenfield, Patricia. *Culture, Concepts and Conservation: A Comparative Study of Cognitive Development in Senegal.* Unpublished doctoral dissertation, Harvard University, 1966a.

————. "On Culture and Conservation." In Jerome Bruner, *et al., Studies in Cognitive Growth.* New York: John Wiley & Sons, Inc., 1966b, pp. 225-256.

————, Reich, Lee, and Olver, Rose. "On Culture and Equivalence: II." In Jerome Bruner *et al., Studies in Cognitive Growth.* New York: John Wiley & Sons, Inc., 1966. pp. 257-315.

Harris, Verona. "Colour Perception and Language." In *Report of Seminar on the Perception of Pictures and Its Relation to Education.* Makerere University College, Kampala, Uganda, 1966.

Haward, L. C. R., and Roland, W. A. "Some Intercultural Differences on the Draw-A-Man Test: III. Conclusion." *Man, 1955, 55,* pp. 40-42.

Hill, Shirley. "Cultural Differences in Mathematical Concept Learning." *American Anthropologist, 1964, 66(2),* pp. 201-222.

Jahoda, Gustav. "Assessment of Abstract Behavior in a Non-Western Culture." *Journal of Abnormal and Social Psychology, 1956, 53,* pp. 237-243.

Lévy-Bruhl, Lucien. *How Natives Think.* London: Allen and Unwin, 1926.

Liddicoat, Renée, and Koza, Constance. "Language Development in African Infants." *Psychologica Africana, 1963, 10,* pp. 108-116.

Mundy-Castle, A. C. *An Experimental Study of Prediction among Ghanaian Children.* Unpublished manuscript, 1966.

Murray, M. *The Development of Spatial Concepts in African and European Children.* Unpublished masters thesis, University of Natal, 1961.

Otaala, Barnabus. *African Children's Thinking about Natural Phenomena.* Unpublished report, Institute of Education, Makerere University College, no date.

Price-Williams, Douglas. "Analysis of an Intelligence Test Used in Rural Areas of Central Nigeria. *Overseas Education,* 1961a, *33,* pp. 124-133.

————. "A Study Concerning Concepts of Conservation of Quantities among Primitive Children." *Acta Psychologica,* 1961b, *18(4),* pp. 297-305.

————. "Abstract and Concrete Modes of Classification in a Primitive Society." *British Journal of Educational Psychology,* 1962, *32,* pp. 50-61.

Raum, Otto F. "The African's Gift for Mathematics." *Overseas Education,* 1933, *5* and 1935, *6.*

Serpell, Robert. "Selective Attention in Children." *Bulletin, Institute of Social Research,* University of Zambia, 1966, *1,* pp. 37-41.

Suchman, Rosslyn. "Cultural Differences in Children's Color and Form Perception." *Journal of Social Psychology,* 1966, *70,* pp. 3-10.

Uka, N. *The Development of Time Concepts in African Children of Primary School Age.* Ibadan: Institute of Education, Occasional Publication No. 3, 1962.

Van Rensenburg, Jansen. *The Learning Ability of the South African Native Compared with That of the European.* Pretoria: South African Council for Education and Social Research. 1933.

Whorf, Benjamin. *Language Thought and Reality: Selected Writings of Benjamin Lee Whorf.* J. B. Carroll (ed.). New York: John Wiley & Sons, Inc., 1956.

VII. Current Research

> The owner of the horse [soon] tells us that his horse is dead,
> how much sooner will the boy who cuts grass for it.
>
> Hausa Proverb

This chapter presents a review of current and proposed research involving the African child, and concludes with a discussion of several bibliographic works which supplement the materials found in this book. Rather than presenting the discussion of current and proposed research according to subject matter, it will be presented according to the foundation or institution supporting the research.

One of the main concerns of the Institute of Education in Tanzania has been the development of curriculum for both secondary and primary pupils. Work is being done in this area by panels of individuals from the Ministry of Education, teachers from various schools throughout the country, including teacher training colleges, and staff from the Institute of Education. Also, within the Institute various individuals are carrying out research projects which will provide information on the development of the African child.

While teaching educational psychology at University College, Dar es Salaam, E. Klingelhofer found that there was no descriptive material on the Tanzanian student, so he began collecting data to provide minimal information in order to better meet the present needs of his students. Klingelhofer collected data on students' interests, abilities, and aptitudes, and also attempted to measure their general intelligence. Specific tests Klingelhofer used were Raven's Progressive Matrices, a modified version of a questionnaire developed by Gillespie and Allport to ascertain information on attitudes and interests, and, at the lower primary level, Goodenough's Draw-A-Man and the Bender Gestalt tests.

Klingelhofer was also interested in collecting data on current values and practices within various tribes in Tanzania in order to: (1) preserve this information during a time when the society is undergoing rapid social change so that later the effects of these changes can be studied; and (2) better understand personality organization within the culture and how it interacts with such variables as family structure, sex, linguistic media, and education.

Although Klingelhofer has completed the collection of his data, it has not as yet been published. However, preliminary reports have been submitted to the University and the Ministry of Education. In his preliminary report,

Klingelhofer discussed the results of work with university and secondary school students. One of the student's interests looked at was occupational goals. His analysis indicated that students were unrealistic in terms of their expectations since they did not mesh with current manpower needs in Tanzania. Although this is not true at all occupational levels, it does suggest that more guidance should be given to pupils in terms of occupational possiblilites within Tanzania.

John Beattie has been concerned with the problems of educational selection at the primary level. He has been developing attainment tests for use at the end of primary school, and has been experimenting with the effects of administering these tests in English and Swahili. The subject matter experimented with has included social studies, science, number skills, and arithmetic reasoning. Beattie's reason for experimenting with the tests in Swahili derives from the fact that performance on many tests may be the result of the child's ability to use the English language, rather than his knowledge of the subject. In devising tests, Beattie is incorporating items which require understanding rather than straight retention of specific information. Beattie's work is extensive, and a considerable amount of testing, analysis, and retesting is being done to create valid and reliable tests.

Two studies in their pilot stage are concerned with the visual perception of African pupils. Charles A. Pratt is working with a committee within the university to devise pictures for use in textbooks in East Africa. In the experiment being designed, 20 different scenes are to be represented by such media as a color photograph, a drawing which duplicates the photograph, and an artist's interpretation of the scene. A selection of these pictures will be presented to children just entering primary school, Standard 4 leavers, Standard 7 leavers, and students in teacher-training colleges. It is hoped that this experiment will provide information on what types of representation are easiest for children to interpret, and will also provide a better understanding of perceptual processes in African children.

Harold Anderson's work began when he discovered that science pupils had difficulty identifying colors correctly. In many sciences it is crucial that colors be recognized in order to carry out observation of phenomena. Pupils appeared to have difficulty in learning when the experience was dependent on differentiation of colors. He then designed a pilot experiment (1967) to answer the following questions: To what extent do color recognition and naming deficiency exist? Do they vary according to academic maturity, general academic ability, color, the various characteristics of color, or tribal background? The pilot test took place in a secondary school in Morogoro, Tanzania, in four classes within the same grade level which represented contrasting abilities as well as differences in academic maturity. Under a highly controlled situation pupils were presented with eight different color discs and asked to record the name of the color.

From the results of the pilot work, Anderson came to the following tentative conclusions: (1) Some secondary school pupils may be handicapped in certain learning tasks because they are unable to correctly recognize and identify colors. However, the "complete inability to identify and differentiate between colors is of very low incidence among the pupils tested" (p. 13). (2) There seems to be a stronger relationship between general academic ability and color identity than between academic maturity and color recognition. (3) Whereas orange and violet are the most difficult to identify, red and blue appear to be most easily identified, followed by yellow and shades of blue and green. (4) The pilot work did not provide adequate data on the difficulties posed by the characteristics of colors. (5) Tribal background does not seem to affect this skill.

At the child development research unit, located at University College, Nairobi, Kenya, investigations into child-rearing practices and child behavior as related to the culture are being carried out by Beatrice and John Whiting in collaboration with other American scholars, as well as with students from the college. Their work involves the comparison of cultures on various dimensions, especially in terms of the effect of a child's socialization by his parents and society on his later social interaction.

The paper the Whitings (1968) presented at the East African social science conference discussed work based on the theoretical assumption that the tasks assigned to and performed by boys and girls during their childhood have an important effect on their style of social behavior. The case in study was developed around the thesis that "boys who are assigned the task of caring for the family learn responsibility or pro-social dominance from performing this duty and their scores on this type of behavior will be higher than those of children who are assigned other tasks, such as performing routine household chores or attending school" (p. 4). Six cultures were then looked at in terms of the importance of herding in the culture and responsibility or pro-social dominance behavior of the boys within the society. A complete report of the Whitings' findings is soon to published in a monograph, *The Behavior of Children in Six Cultures.*

The proceedings of the seminar on research methods held at Makerere University College, Kampala, Uganda, in August 1967, includes a section written by Hamed El-Abd summarizing the current and proposed research interests within the Faculty of Education at Makerere. Work has recently been completed on various methods which may be suitably used in selection procedures. An experiment was carried out with a group of refugees, twelve of whom were to be given further education. Testing involved both intelligence tests and sociometric ratings by the group. The results suggest that the more teachers are able to observe and get to know the children they teach, the better they are able to assess the children's ability. Also, teachers could usefully employ an interview technique to form a reliable opinion of a child.

El-Abd has also done some comparative studies among students at Makerere. For example, he administered the Otis Higher Examination to both African and British Diploma of Education students. He concluded that scores on this test are influenced by the subject's reading ability, his excellence in using English, and his experience in using similar materials. El-Abd undertook still another study, which was designed to ascertain whether the facets of mental ability found in Western cultures applied to the African setting. A battery of tests was given to Bachelor of Education students at Makerere, from which he concluded that the structure of intelligence is the same in Western and African cultures. However, it is easier for a Westerner to score higher on standard intelligence tests because the tests were devised within his culture. When the Western child is young he has access to the materials used on the tests. On the other hand, the African child has little or no contact with these materials and is thus handicapped when asked to perform tasks with unfamiliar items.

Another experiment involved the use of programmed learning texts in geography, in which a set of programmed texts was used with an experimental and a control group from a Form I class in one of the secondary schools in Uganda. A pre-test and two forms of a general ability test were administered at the beginning of the program, and an objective test was set at the end of the course. The results of tests at the completion of the course indicated no significant difference in test scores between the two groups. However, after a school holiday, pupils were told they would be retested on the same material. They were given their books but not provided with a review of the material during class time. When retested, the pupils who worked under the programmed instruction course scored significantly higher than those in the control group.

Barnabus Otaala is investigating the stages of thinking of Ugandan African children. He is operating on the assumption that the developmental trend of thinking in African children will follow Piaget's stages of development. The experiment is being carried out among children aged six to eleven from a rural and an urban school in Teso, a district of Uganda. The pilot work in this project was carried out in September 1967. A new testing program began in June 1968 to follow up many ideas suggested by the earlier testing.

Other areas the Faculty is interested in exploring include: (1) the construction of a general mental ability test to be used in the selection of Uganda primary school children for further education; (2) building up norms for the Lule Multi-Racial Picture Intelligence Test; (3) application of the Minnesota Teacher Attitude Inventory to East Africans; (4) the personality of the East African B.Ed. student as measured by Cattell's 16 Personality Questionnaire; (5) validation of a scale for measuring teacher attitudes toward discipline in Uganda; and (6) the cognition of behavioral figures – a study of human faces.

Lorene Fox has spent the last two years compiling a book of readings in psychology that can be used in teacher training colleges in East Africa. These readings include various research works carried out in Western cultures that have implications in other cultural settings as well. Where possible, references have been included which refer to work actually done in Africa.

Paul Mayerson is engaged in a study of reading comprehension to see if it can be taught more effectively in primary schools. For his experiment, Mayerson has devised two comparable tests for pre- and post-testing which evaluate reading comprehension. He is administering the Science Research Associates Reading Laboratory IIa to selected P VI classes and will compare the test scores of children who have had this course with the scores of a control group. It is hoped that this study will provide some guidelines for designing better programs for the teaching of English in primary schools in Uganda.

During the summer of 1967, the Institute of Education, Makerere University College, in conjunction with Teachers College, Columbia University, sponsored three research projects in Uganda. These were headed by personnel from Teachers College, and were designed to explore different aspects of child growth and development in Africa.

Millie Almy (1967) did several studies on the use of Piagetian techniques with P I and P III classes in Kampala. The specific tasks employed were conservation, classification, seriation, and direction. Basically, the format used in the standardized version of these tasks was followed, but many of the materials were changed to make the task applicable for Baganda children. In her summary, Almy stated that the children are largely "preoperational" in their thinking processes:

> Their thinking appears to impressionistic and unsystematic, untroubled by logical contradiction. To a considerable extent they are beguiled by the appearance of things, interested in small details, likely to pay attention to differences about as often as to similarities, and are more interested in color than form (p. 21).

Some questions raised by Almy's work are: (1) Does language bear any relationship to the way the children respond in the interviews? (2) Are the abilities involved in classification, seriation, and the understanding of space relationships developing at different rates? (3) How pervasive is the children's interest in color? (4) If, as the present study suggests, conservation of number is not generally established by P III, when is it achieved? (5) What are the typical pre-school experiences for Baganda children? Answers to these will have a direct bearing on curriculum at the primary level.

Joel Davitz was involved in two studies. One was a study of children's emotional experiences, the other of productive thinking. The 107 subjects in the first study ranged from 12 to 20 years of age. They were asked to describe emotional experiences of happiness, sadness, and anger as fully as possible, and the events which caused them. The subjects were given their choice of responding in English or Luganda. The experiences which most often initiated feelings of happiness were connected with academic success, and were characterized by expressive behavior and a sense of activation. Sadness was almost always associated with the death of a parent, sibling, or close relative, and typically characterized by the desire to be alone. The descriptions of sadness are particularly rich in detail compared to those of American students. Anger was brought about by an attack from an adult or another child. The children responded with aggressive feelings acted out against other children, but not adults. In relationships with adults, children appeared to be overtly passive and emotionally unexpressive, yet their responses reveal that they are sensitive and have strong emotional reactions.

In Davitz's (1967) study on productive thinking, pupils were presented with an interview schedule which consisted of five sections: (1) naming examples within general categories; (2) alternative uses of common objects; (3) similarities between objects; (4) interpretations of possible meanings of various graphic patterns; (5) interpretations of possible meanings of various line drawings (p. 16). Analysis of the results indicated that the children were most productive in giving instances of general categories and alternative uses of objects, and least productive in response to graphic stimuli. Also, there was a great diversity in the children's ability to express themselves in English. Davitz concluded his report with some recommendations for educational practice based on these findings.

Mary Alice White (1967), using 306 children from P III–P VII, studied their understanding of their school as a system. Do children understand the system, what it demands of them, and how to operate within the system to maximize rewards? The technique used has been termed "teaching exchanges." In these exhanges two pupils from one grade level attempt to teach something to two students from the grade below. Two factors which made this technique difficult in the Ugandan setting were the children's difficulty in using English with ease, and their lack of spontaneity in front of adults. White found that: (1) the children clearly understand how the school works, what it stresses in the curriculum, its marking system, and the system of rewards and punishments; (2) the reward and punishment system in the home is consistent with that of the school in terms of school learning; (3) greater emphasis, in both the home and the school, is placed on academic achievement than on agricultural occupations; (4) the pupils appear to have a limited repertoire of learning techniques, which may be due to language, culture, and classroom practices; (5) the school as a system is clear and consistent. White then raised the question of the relevance of the existing system for the current needs of Uganda.

In 1967 Syracuse University received a grant from the Carnegie Corporation to carry out a cross-cultural research training program with teaching and research facilities at Makerere University College. The purposes of the program are to: (1) train graduate students in cross-cultural research; (2) establish a psychology department at Makerere; (3) provide graduate training in psychology for African students; and (4) provide a continuation of joint research between Syracuse and Makerere. The emphasis of this research program is on discovering the

form and content and perceptual processes characteristic of the peoples of Africa with the over-all goal of such research being an increment of understanding, in terms of Western social-scientific frames of reference, of the psychology of these and possibly other, non-Western peoples (Segall, 1967).

The ultimate goal of the project is to develop a group of African pyschologists who can both teach and do research in Africa.

Some of the research completed in 1968 under the sponsorship of Makerere's department of social psychology includes that of Segall, Richard Kingsley, and Mira Schiff. Others who worked closely in conjunction with the department are Nancy Graves and this author.

Schiff's project deals with the relationship between children's curiosity and child-rearing practices in Uganda. It was hypothesized that the child-rearing practices found within traditional Buganda may suppress a child's overt curiosity. The four aspects of curiosity explored were: (1) verbal questioning, (2) exploration – the active seeking of new stimuli and materials, (3) investigation – learning about the new stimuli and experiences, and (4) manipulation – handling the materials to learn how they are made and how they work. Through interviews, Schiff sought to acquire background information on the families and their child-rearing practices to get an idea of the types of experiences and stimulation provided in the home. Questions were also directed at ascertaining the mothers' attitudes toward the four types of curiosity described above. By using a standard interview with the mothers and observing the interaction between mother and child when the latter was presented with a "curiosity box" and other toys, Schiff made an assessment of the amount of curiosity exhibited by the child and the effect of the interaction between the child and mother in terms of whether it encouraged or inhibited curiosity.

One important dimension in Schiff's study dealt with the level of acculturation. Other studies of the Ganda indicate that traditional child-rearing practices emphasize obedience, whereas European-influenced Ganda are more permissive and approve of exploration by their children. The results of Schiff's study indicate that both the mother's and the child's behavior is related to acculturation level. Traditional mothers actively discourage the child from asking questions and exploring. The child of the traditional mother is therefore passive and scores low on autonomy ratings. The study indicates that culture plays a large part in the extent to which a child will undertake the exploration of his environment; experience establishes habits related to how to deal with novelty, the search for new information, and patterns of learning (Segall, 1968, p.7).

Another researcher looking at child-rearing practices and mother-child interactions was Nancy Graves. Her study was part of a larger one in which three cultural groups were being compared: lower-income rural and urban Spanish-American; lower-income urban Anglo-American; and lower-income urban and rural Ganda families. Graves' research was concerned with maternal attitudes and child-rearing practices, and the effect that acculturation and urbanization may have on them. In working with the Ganda, interviews with 30 urban and 30 rural families were held. Then ten families in each group were studied more intensively in terms of child-rearing methods and attitudes. This was accomplished by observations in the home during three visits and included an interview with the mother concerning her child-rearing practices. The last phase involved interviewing the fathers along the same measures used with the mothers, and making an intensive case-study of two or three families. Preliminary results indicate that Ganda mothers are not acculturating to European models to any significant extent. This may be resultant from the fact that Ganda mothers are not in contact with Europeans enough to be under direct acculturative pressure.

Three studies just completed deal with the way children develop concepts and the types they develop. Richard Kingsley did two studies of "single-dimensional and two-dimensional" discrimination performance in Uganda in an effort to relate it to the manner in which children form categories and concepts. This writer's work involved trying to teach children the concepts of grouping by color and by function.

In Kingsley's first study children were taught to sort objects into two categories on the basis of either of two possible dimensions. They were then required to find another way to sort the objects. For some this involved sorting on the same dimension but reversing its direction (reversal shift), for the others sorting by the third dimension presented in the stimuli (extra-dimensional shift). The results indicated that young Ugandan children find discrimination easier to learn where a shape rather than a color is reinforced. Also, when required to learn a different cue, children transfer from one shape to another faster than from shape to color, or color to shape. Older children seemed to learn both the reversal and extra-dimensional shifts with equal ease (1968).

The results of the first experiment suggested avenues that Kingsley explored in a second, in which he found that neither color nor shape preferences appear to be related to age, and that age is not a factor in determining the number of errors made in reversing on the color dimension. Younger children find it more difficult to learn shape reversals than color reversals, but with increasing age it becomes as easy.

Several studies in both Western and African cultures have found that when children are presented with familiar stimuli and asked to sort them, color is the most salient feature to the child; sorting by function is infrequent. This is particularly true in studies of African cultures. In these studies the subject was instructed to match like ojbects in a free choice, open-ended situation.

This writer's experiment, with Segall (1968, 1969), on the other hand, was an attempt to see what concepts could be taught to children at various age levels. Differential ease of learning was the index used to represent the subject's ability to use color and function for equivalence grouping. The subjects for the experiment were pupils from three schools in Uganda (urban, urban-rural, rural) in P I, P III, and P V. Also included was a group of 40 children who had not attended school or who had only attended school through P III, and a group of adults who never attended school, half living in Kampala, the other half living about 50 miles from the city. All subjects in the experiment were given the opportunity to learn to sort pictures of familiar objects on two different bases of equivalence grouping: color and function. Half were presented first with color, then function, while the other half learned in the reverse order.

The basic findings of the study were that: (1) Sorting by color was learned more rapidly than sorting by function by most subjects. This was indicated by the number of trials necessary to attain the designated criterion for learning and by the number of subjects who failed to reach criterion. (2) Performance in sorting by function improved significantly as a function of years in school; children in P V performed both tasks with equal ease. (3) Age alone could not account for improvement in the ability to sort by function, since older unschooled children and adults who had only minimal schooling (less than P III) had as much difficulty learning to sort by function as did younger school children.

These findings suggest that color is a more easily identified dimension, and that unless the child is asked to use another basis for equivalence grouping, or has a tendency to look for the less obvious – a tendency reinforced by some experiences – color remains dominant. P V children in the study had such a tendency. It was also true that urban children exhibited the tendency more frequently than rural children. We concluded that the development of cognitive processes is not solely the result of intellectual maturity; it is dependent upon experience.

Another study in which Segall (1968) was involved examined the relationship between language structure and the way it may hinder or facilitate learning. In the Bantu languages nouns are prefixed in order to indicate singular or plural, whereas in English words are suffixed, usually with "s." In order to study the possible effects of Bantu prefixes on a concept-discovery problem, children were randomly assigned to two different groups. A child in Group A was told he was going to be shown things called MIKALO and MAKALO and that he had to learn which objects went into which group. Group B was informed that things they were to be shown were to go into groups called KALOMA and KALOMI. The difference in the group names is a function of where the MA and MI are placed. The stimuli presented to the children varied in number and form and could be sorted either way. Half the children were randomly assigned to be reinforced for sorting on the basis of number, and half on the basis of form. The experiment was designed to test the prediction that children who speak a Bantu language would find sorting by number easier when the groups they use are labelled MAKALO and MIKALO, and when sorting by form children would find the task easier if their groups are KALOMA and KALOMI. It was also predicted that children able to use English easily would perform the tasks with equal ease (pp. 10-11). The experiment was conducted with Ankole and Ganda children between the ages of seven and eleven. A preliminary investigation of the data reveals the predicted interaction between grouping and class names. From this study Segall concluded:

> Whatever else may have acted to assist or detract from the subjects' efforts to discover what they were supposed to do, the position of two syllables in the instructions had an effect on their thought processes. . . . The experiment demonstrated that what a thing was to be called influenced how it was processed conceptually (p.12).

Segall thus emphasizes the importance of psycholinguistics in understanding more about the relationship between thought and language.

Besides the work which Schiff is doing with pre-school children, further work is being done to study the effects of nursery school on children. One measure devised included time-sampling observations of the children — recording all they do and say within specified time units. Another is a test of language development, in which each child is tested twice, once in English and once in his native language early and later in his nursery school experience. Preliminary results indicate that children tested in their mother tongue during the first weeks of nursery school have scores comparable to those of European children tested in English. This indicates that the content of the test is appropriate for the children being tested. Another research finding that would be interesting to pursue is that Luganda-speaking children sometimes respond to a test item in English and claim not to know the comparable Luganda. This suggests that they may have difficulty in moving from one language to another when referring to certain events learned in or about one language rather than in another.

Segall has already done a considerable amount of research on the African's perceptual difficulties (see Segall, Campbell, and Herskovits, 1966, *The Influence of Culture on Visual Perception*), and is interested in further exploring such questions as: Do people have trouble interpreting a photograph? If so, what are the characteristics of these people? Which depth cues in pictures and photographs are not easily perceived? Is a picture easier to interpret in black-and-white or in color, or does it make no difference? (Segall, 1967, p. 14). It is also hoped that various aspects of perceptual constancy can be studied cross-culturally.

Research has indicated that personality and motive affect one's perception. Employing a stereoscope, an optical apparatus which permits the presentation of a different picture to each eye, Segall plans to present children with a series of paired pictures and have them report what they see. One picture will represent a violent scene, while the other will present a serene one. Generally, the viewer reports the scene which is most salient to him. A stereoscope can also be used to present subjects with both a familiar stimuli and a unique one to help answer the question: Does familiarity with the object affect perception?

Currently Segall is in the process of writing up a study on acculturation and the hopes and aspirations of secondary school boys in Uganda. Data for this study was collected in 1959, through funds from the Carnegie Corporation, when junior and senior secondary pupils in Ankole were asked to write essays and complete questionnaires relating to their future.

Several departments within Makerere are cooperating in an investigation into the effects of malnutrition on maturation and cerebral functioning. Research to date indicates that malnutrition in early life may cause permanent interference in the normal physical and cognitive growth pattern. However, German (1968) maintains that in these studies there were inadequate controls in terms of other variables – in particular, poor family background – which may also affect intellectual functioning. For this reason the group at Makerere hopes to explore the following questions: (1) Is it possible to separate the effects of malnutrition from the effects of emotional deprivation? (2) If malnutrition is established as a cause of poor psychological development, then what is the exact nature of that deficit? Can it be measured in terms of brain function? (3) How permanent is the deficit? and (4) If a deficit continues into adult life, what are its manifestations?

The first phase of the study will involve searching out documented cases of malnutrition who reported to the Medical Research Council Infantile Malnutrition Unit ten to twelve years ago. The second phase will include extensive testing of these children as well as control groups. Included in the battery of tests will be: psychometric evaluation, personality assessment, nutritional and physical assessments, and E.E.G. recordings.

The University of Malawi, established in 1964, has done some research with children in that country. A questionnaire used in Rhodesia (see report of work by Alec Thompson, University College, Rhodesia) was administered to primary school children in Malawi by students in an educational psychology course. The purposes of the study were to learn something about children's toys and to train education students in research methods. Among the questions were: What is your favorite toy? How long have you had it? Was the toy bought or handmade? If it was handmade, who made it? How long did it take to make the toy? Does it have any moving parts? What would you like to have if you could have any toy you wanted? Analysis of the data was then done by the students who made a display using graphs to summarize the results.

Further research plans include giving a battery of tests to children at the end of primary school to better assess their knowledge and general intelligence levels. It is also hoped that a pre-university course will be established for potential university entrants. During the summer before students begin their first year they will attend the university for a series of courses and take a battery of intelligence and psychological tests. These will be analyzed and the students assigned to the branch of the university which best fits their capabilities. In this way they can be realistically guided in career choices in accordance with the manpower needs of the country and their own potential.

The Institute of Social Research in Zambia, formerly the Rhodes-Livingstone Institute, is currently under the direction of Alastair Heron. The research interests of the institute at present are reflected in a series of monographs issued under the name of the Human Development Research Unit. The works of Serpell and Deregowski have been included.

Deregowski has centered his work on visual perception in children, asking such questions as: What are some of the variables which affect perception? Are Africans susceptible to perceptual illusions in the same way that Europeans are? Are children able to use depth cues in a picture? What type of cues are of the greatest help? From his work to date Deregowski has concluded that African children do not have general perceptual difficulties, rather, their ability to interpret pictures depends on the picture itself, the instructions given, and the task required. Some types of pictures are more difficult to interpret. Deregowski also believes that the ability to interpret pictures is connected with the child's educational experiences, and that mental, rather than chronological, age is the determinant of perceptual tasks. Deregowski is continuing his work on perception, part of which is the exploration of factors within the environment which may affect perception.

Serpell's work (1966) has revolved around the question of selective attention in children. In other words, what features within the stimuli are important in helping children to focus on the object? In a series of experiments, Serpell has varied the intensity and recognizability of such dimensions as color and form. In general, the influence of the stimulus appears to be the result of the degree of difference between the alternatives presented for comparison. By using the materials with different groups of children he has also made some hypotheses about the effect of schooling on specific tasks.

As well as doing basic research in the areas of perceptual and cognitive development, members of the Institute in Lusaka have been interested in the development of task motivation. In a series of studies Munro is looking at four measures of task-related motivation in primary school children: (1) performance, (2) perseverance, (3) level of aspiration, and (4) general behavior on a specific task. At present he is involved in the development of valid instruments within the Zambian population.

In August 1967, the Faculty of Education at University College, Salisbury, Rhodesia, produced a pamphlet of individual interests and research projects within the faculty. Elizabeth Hendrikz's present interests revolve around child development, with particular reference to the effects of culture, environment, and socio-economic levels as they relate to intellectual development. It is expected that the results of such inquiries will provide guidelines for school curriculum revision and new teaching methods. Hendrikz is particularly interested in how the above factors relate to mathematics and the sciences.

Her previous research in Rhodesia (1965) included an investigation into number concepts and the level of number development in five-year-old European and Shona children, in which she attempted to assess children's development and provide validation for Piaget-type theories of intellectual development. The format of the interview was a shortened version of Piaget's experiments, which was administered to 304 children in Rhodesia. The specific areas were: (1) conservation of discrete quantity, (2) classification, (3) one-to-one correspondence, (4) seriation, (5) addition and the ability to "count-on," (6) enumeration, and (7) knowledge of number symbols. Her work suggested that the European child is superior on conceptual tasks; that children of both races with nursery school experience are at a more advanced level conceptually than non-nursery school children; that boys tend to do better than girls, but the difference is not significant; and that there is a relationship between the ability to count, read numbers and do mechanical addition, and the level of the children's mathematical conceptual development. Hendrikz concluded that there is a significant difference in the level of intellectual development attained by African and European school children, but that any such difference can be accounted for by cultural and environmental variations.

Currently Hendrikz is involved in two research projects. One is a cross-cultural investigation into the development of mathematical thinking at the early adolescent level with upper primary school children. The other is in conjunction with a medical team attempting to assess the effects of bilharzia (schistosomiasis) on the intellectual growth of children.

S. F. W. Orbell (1967) has been interested in children's classification performance and rationale. In his pilot work he presented children with 40 simple objects which represented a large variety of stimuli. Each child was asked to examine the objects and then put them in groups which seemed to belong together. Orbell's work has shown that the more remote and isolated a group of subjects is, the more concrete and less abstract are the subjects' definitions for groups. Orbell interviewed twelve-year-old urban children who had attended seven years of school. He is still looking for a meaningful way to assess classifications which occur within indigenous societies.

Orbell has also done some research on color perception. He has found that children have trouble distinguishing between pink and purple, brown and red, yellow and orange, and yellow and white. It may well be that this is partly a function of the Bantu languages, which do not provide names for many of the colors we distinguish in English. Orbell found that the Shona people have the same word for blue and green, and that their word for brown also stands for red. Further work needs to be done in this area in terms of the effects of language upon concept learning and the way in which the indigenous language affects the learning of other languages.

Michael Robson is interested in the effect of language on the development of science concepts, both in terms of what the child brings with him conceptually from his own language, and the effects of a child's ability to use English on his understanding of science. In devising new textbooks, Robson is concerned with teaching children how to use pictures, since this ability is essential in reading science materials.

Alec Thompson (1967) became interested in the intricacies of children's toys, especially toy cars made from wire. A census of children's toys was initiated, not only to discover the children's favorite toys and playthings, but also to collect some simple statistics about the toys. An analysis showed that actual and wishful ownership have distributions among children by age and by sex, peculiar to each kind of toy. In diminishing order of frequency, the toys which boys made for themselves are wheeled toys, weapons, toy animals, musical instruments, and balls. Girls are more restricted in the types of toys they make for themselves, their playthings being chiefly dolls and balls. Further analysis of children's toys is planned, as it may be an indication of children's ability to create, manipulate, and use various materials (pp. 3-7).

In 1960, Ibadan University in Nigeria produced a draft development plan to cover the years 1961-1970. In the area of educational research the following three areas were to be considered: A. child growth and development; B. curriculum studies and research in: (1) language, (2) time and space concepts, (3) concepts of natural phenomena, and (4) arithmetic and mathematics; and C. history and sociology of education – the sociological determinants of educational policy. Since 1961 work has been done on measuring tests and interviewing and recording techniques, and students have been involved in studies on child training, case studies, children's language and lore, games, songs, stories, and interests. This work has been under the direction of N. Uka.

During the last six years the Institute of Child Health has been involved in a longitudinal study of two groups within the Yoruba tribe. The group referred to as "Oje" represents children whose parents follow traditional patterns and are currently living in the Oje district in Ibadan. The second group, the "elite," is composed of children whose parents received a Western education.

One aspect of this study has been the recording of the children's physical development. Janes (1967) reports consistent differences between the two groups, with the elite equalling or surpassing European norms, while the Oje children are typically behind at each stage of development.

Abiola (1965) has worked on the development of a mental measurement scale and has applied it to the longitudinal sample described above. His results have been surprising in that he found that the difference between the Oje and elite is curvilinear. Children were tested at ages one, three, and five. The two groups were similar at ages one and five; the elite scored significantly higher than the Oje at age three (p. 5).

Knowledge of the children's environment would suggest there should be the large difference at age three, as found, but it would also suggest that by age five the differences would have increased since the environment of the elite group would continue to provide them with experiences which would supposedly aid their intellectual development. The Oje, on the other hand, would have none of these experiences. Abiola suggests that further research should be done to study the development of the Oje child between the ages of three and five, as well as the apparent decrease in score between the ages of three and five of the elite child.

The intellectual development of this group is being further explored by Barbara Lloyd (1968). Basically she is using three techniques: (a) intelligence tests, (2) Piagetian tasks, and (3) oddity problem solving. In intelligence testing she is using Form L-M of the Stanford Binet. Lloyd hypothesizes that the greatest difference in performance will occur on items which are not easily translatable into Yoruba. In other words, children who have had experience with items related specifically to European life will be more familiar with the tasks and thus will perform better. The Piagetian tasks being used involve number, discrete and continuous quantity, class, and seriation. On these tasks Lloyd is looking specifically at the patterns of learning across tasks. In oddity problem solving the child must choose the "odd" stimulus from among three objects. As well as recording the child's performance, the experimenter will observe the child while he is learning. Lloyd predicts there will be little difference in performance among those who are able to do the task. However, she predicts that the Oje group will have greater difficulty verbally describing their performance.

Other works being done in Ibadan are as follows: a paper by T. Hunter on child-training procedures in Chitsha and an article by Lloyd on some observations of child training among the Hausa are in press; R. H. Stone is exploring the concepts of natural phenomena among Yoruba children, and the area of curriculum; E. A. Yoloye is developing a primary school science program in Western Nigeria.

The Institute of Education in Ghana has also been interested in research with young children. The report produced in 1960, written by Andrew Taylor and Barington-Kaye, was largely a discussion of current and proposed work of the Child Development Research Unit. Due to the lack of adequate materials on traditional child-rearing practices and the effects of a changing society on the growth of children, a systematic and integrative survey of motor, intellectual, emotional, social, and aesthetic growth studies were proposed. The specific objectives of the program were to identify and describe: (1) growth patterns characteristic of each stage of the life cycle; (2) social pressures which influence the development of knowledge, competency, behavior, attitudes, and aspirations in children; (3) the social roles which the society permits the child; (4) the educational and social significance of individual differences among children; (5) the interaction of social and self-mediated processes as they shape the motivation of the child in a particular situation, and as the total personality of the child develops through time; (6) internal motivations and how their satisfaction or frustration influences the child; (7) the traditional methods of problem solving and conceptual growth; and (8) the growth of social consciousness with particular reference to citizenship and the development of techniques aimed at developing desirable attitudes toward self, social activity, and social responsibility.

It was proposed that these studies should be carried out cross-sectionally and longitudinally over a period of 18 years. The first project, to last five years, was divided into three major areas: Medical, Anthropological, and Psychological.

Due to the broadness of the term "psychological," several areas which are parts of the discipline have not been included in this book. For this reason it concludes with a review of several bibliographies which supplement the material discussed in this work. The bibliographies included have been divided into three sections: education, psychology, and general.

Works on education in Africa. Margaret Couch's (1962, 1965) bibliographies include references on all phases of education in Africa. They are organized by country and subdivided into various institutes. Couch's bibliographies are not annotated, nor is the bibliography by Yates (1964), whose work deals with problems of education in Africa South of the Sahara and is somewhat more focused than the works by Couch.

Howard Drake's bibliography (1942) includes sections on the then current material related to African education in general and on the social and political implications of education and educational policy as affected by governmental, religious, agricultural, and vocational considerations. It also contains sections on the training of teachers, the development of education programs for adults, and the education of women and children.

A very valuable reference book on education in Africa is the work of J. W. Hanson and G. W. Gibson (1966). It is annotated and provides materials from 1960 to 1966 which reflect the recent development of education within African countries.

Works on psychology in Africa. Psychological bibliographies include the works of Doob, Biesheuvel, Verhaegen and Laroch, Crijns, Klingelhofer, Andor, Hopkins, and Wickert. Doob's (1960) chapter on psychology provides an overview of psychology in Africa and contains a comprehensive bibliography. It includes references on psychiatric problems and psychological analyses which have not been included in this book.

The works of Biesheuvel (1958a, b) and Verhaegen and Laroch (1958), whose discussion of research methodology in Africa is included in the chapter on intelligence, contain references on psychological research in Africa and in other cultures.

Crijn's works (1962, 1966) provide bibliographic references to specific areas of psychology. His earlier work contains references to studies on African intelligence, and the latter includes a summary of materials written about the African personality structure. Both works are critical reviews of the literature.

Klingelhofer (1967) produced a bibliography which includes the following areas of psychology: experimental, physiological, developmental, social, personality and abilities, therapy and guidance, abnormal, educational, and industrial and military psychology. His work contains materials from a wide variety of sources and is quite valuable in this respect. Klingelhofer has not reviewed any of the materials contained in his bibliography. The annotated bibliography of Andor (1966) is more specific in that it contains only studies of the African's abilities and aptitudes.

Hopkins' bibliography (1962) contains references to articles written in French not contained in this book. Wickert has translated articles from French into English, and has included sections of these articles in his excellent collection of readings.

References in the general category. In his bibliography, Dipeolu (1966) restricted himself geographically to Nigeria. His work has been compiled mainly for the individual interested in doing research in that country. The references included are annotated. R.M.S. Ng'ombe (1957) has also restricted himself to a geographical region: Rhodesia and Nyasaland. His work is complete on research in all fields. Reader's work (1961) is limited in that it contains only references to work done in the National Institute of Personnel Research. The Institute has done research on, among other things, intelligence, job training, and manpower requirements, and Reader's article provides a summary of this work.

BIBLIOGRAPHY

Abiola, E. T. "The Nature of Intellectual Development in Nigerian Children." *Teacher Education,* 1965, *6,* pp. 37-58.

Almy, Millie. "The Usefulness of Piagetian Methods for Early Primary Education in Uganda: An Exploratory Study." In *Child Growth and Development Projects,* National Institute of Education, Makerere University College, Kampala, Uganda, 1967.

————, Davitz, Joel R., and White, Mary Alice. *Ugandan Children in School: Four Experimental Studies in Psychology.* New York: Teachers College Press, 1970.

Anderson, Harold. *An Investigation of Color Recognition among Secondary School Students in Tanzania: Report of the Pilot Study.* Institute of Education, University College, Dar es Salaam, Tanzania, 1967.

Andor, L. E. *Aptitudes and Abilities of the Black Man in Sub-Saharan Africa, 1784-1963.* National Institute of Personnel Research, Johannesburg, 1966.

Beattie, John. "Educational Research in East Africa." In *Report of a Seminar in Research Methods Held in the Institute.* National Institute of Education, Makerere University College, Kampala, Uganda, 1967.

————, and Klitzke, Louis. "Occupational Preferences of Tanzanian Students." *Tanzanian Educational Journal,* 1967, *9*(3), pp. 10-12.

————. "Objectives and Methods of African Psychological Research." *Journal of Social Psychology,* 1958a, *47,* pp. 161-168.

Biesheuvel, Simon. "Methodology in the Study of Attitudes of Africans." *Journal of Social Psychology,* 1958b, *47,* pp. 169-184.

Couch, Margaret. *Education in Africa: A Selected Bibliography.* London: Institute of Education, 1962.

————. *Education in Africa: A Select Bibliography, Part II.* London: Institute of Education, 1965.

Crijns, Arthur. "African Intelligence: A Critical Survey of Cross-Cultural Intelligence Research in Africa South of the Sahara." *Journal of Social Psychology,* 1962, *57,* pp. 283-301.

————. "African Personality Structure: A Critical Review of Bibliographical Sources and of Principle Findings." *Gawein,* 1966, *14*(4), pp. 239-248.

Davitz, Joel. "Report on Research in Child Growth and Development." In *Child Growth and Development Projects,* National Institute of Education, Makerere University College, Kampala, Uganda, 1967.

Department of Educational Psychology, Makerere University College. *Draft Proposals for Child Study Research Project.* Kampala, Uganda, 1966.

Deregowski, Jan. *Difficulties in Pictorial Perception in Africa.* Human Development Research Unit, Institute of Social Research, University of Zambia, 1966a, No. 1.

————. *Influence of Perspective upon Perception of Pictorially Represented Volume in Bantu Schoolboys.* Human Development Research Unit, Institute of Social Research, University of Zambia, 1966b, No. 3.

————. *Horizontal-Vertical Illusion and the Ecological Hypothesis.* Human Research Development Unit, Institute of Social Research, University of Zambia, 1967, No. 4.

Dipeolu. *Bibliographical Sources for Nigerian Studies.* Ibadan University, Ibadan, Nigeria, 1966.

Doob, Leonard. "Psychology." In *The African World: A Survey of Social Research,* R. A. Lystad (ed.). London: Pall Mall Press, 1965, pp. 373-415 and 543-549.

Drake, Howard. *A Bibliography of African Education.* University of Aberdeen Anthropological Museum Publication No. 2, 1942.

El-Abd, Hamed. "Educational Psychology Research in the Faculty of Education." In *Report of a Seminar in Research Methods Held in the Institute.* National Institute of Education, Makerere University College, Kampala, Uganda, 1967.

Evans, Judith. *Color and Concept Learning among Baganda Children.* Paper presented at the East African Social Science Conference, Dar es Salaam, Tanzania, January, 1968.

————, and Segall, Marshall. "Learning to Classify by Color and by Function: A Study of Concept-Discovery by Ganda Children." *Journal of Social Psychology,* 1969, 77, pp. 35-53.

German, Allen. *Malnutrition and Long Term Problems of Development.* Paper presented at the Makerere Institute of Social Research Workshop on Social Psychological Research in Africa. New York, 1968.

Graves, Nancy. *Culture, the City, and Child Rearing.* Kampala: Makerere Institute of Social Research, 1968.

Hanson, John, and Gibson, G. W. *A Select and Annotated Bibliography.* Institute for International Studies in Education and The African Studies Center, Michigan State University, 1966.

Hendrikz, Elizabeth. *A Cross-Cultural Investigation of the Number Concepts and Level of Number Development in Five-Year-Old Urban Shona and European Children in Southern Rhodesia.* Unpublished masters thesis, Unversity of London, 1965.

Hopkins, J. "Bibliographie de Recherches Psychologiques Conduites en Afrique." *Revue de Psychologie Appliquée,* 1962, *12,* pp. 201-213.

Individual Interest and Research Projects within the Faculty of Education. University College, Salisbury, Southern Rhodesia, 1967.

Janes, M.D. "Report on Growth and Development Study on Yoruba Children in Ibadan, Western Nigeria." In *Living Conditions of the Child in Rural Environments in Africa.* Paris: Centre International de L'Enfance, 1967, pp. 104-109.

Kingsley, Richard. *Reversal and Extra-Dimensional Shifts by Ugandan Children Using One-Dimensional and Two-Dimensional Discrimination Problems.* Paper presented at the East African Social Science Conference, Dar es Salaam, Tanzania, January 1968.

————. *Culture and Cognitive Style.* Paper presented at the African Studies Association, Los Angeles, 1968.

Klingelhofer, E. L. *A Bibliography of Psychological Research and Writings on Africa.* Uppsala: Scandanavian Institute of African Studies, 1967a.

————. *Studies of Tanzanian Students.* University College, Dar es Salaam, Tanzania, 1967b.

————. *Suggestions for Psychological Research in Africa.* Paper presented at the Makerere Institute of Social Research Workshop on Social Psychological Research in Africa. New York, 1968.

LeVine, Robert. "Cross-Cultural Study in Child Psychology." In *Carmichael's Manual of Child Psychology,* Paul H. Mussen (ed.). New York: John Wiley & Sons, in press.

Lloyd, Barbara. *Antecedents of Personality and Ability Differences in Yoruba Children.* Paper presented at the Makerere Institute of Social Research Workshop on Social Psychological Research in Africa. New York, 1968.

Munro, Donald. *The Development of Task Motivation and Values in Zambia.* Paper presented at the Makerere Institute of Social Research Workshop on Social Psychological Research in Africa. New York, 1968.

Ng'ombe, R. M. S. *A Selected Bibliography of the Federation of Rhodesia and Nyasaland.* Rhodes-Livingstone Communication, No. 7, 1957.

Orbell, S. F. W. "The Object Sorting Test." *Science Education Bulletin* (Salisbury), 1967, *1*(2), p. 5.

Reader. "African and Afro-European Research: A Summary of Previously Unpublished Findings in the National Institute of Personnel Research." *Psychologica Africana,* 1961, *10*, pp. 1-18.

"Report of the Afro-Anglo American Conference, 1965." *Teacher Education,* 1965, *7*(1).

Report on Research. University College, Dar es Salaam, Tanzania, 1967,

Robson, Michael. "Progress Report – the Baird and Tatlock Projects." *Science Education Bulletin* (Salisbury), 1967, *1*(1), pp. 8-13.

Schiff, Mira. *Manifest Curiosity in Baganda Children.* Paper presented at the East African Social Science Conference, Dar es Salaam, Tanzania, January 1968.

————. *Some Consequences of Child-Rearing Practices among the Ganda.* Paper presented at the African Studies Association, Los Angeles, 1968.

Segall, Marshall. *The Makerere Program in Social Psychology: An Overview of Research in Progress.* 1966.

————. *Some Remarks on the Growth of Psychology in African Studies.* Paper presented on the Occasion of the Twentieth Anniversary of the African Studies Program at Northwestern University. Chicago, September 1968.

Serpell, Robert. "Selective Attention in Children." *Bulletin of the Institute for Social Research,* University of Zambia, 1966, *1*, pp. 37-41.

————. *Selective Attention in Matching from Samples by Children.* Human Development Research Unit, Institute for Social Research, University of Zambia, 1966, No. 3.

Thompson, Alec. "Children and Their Toys." *Science Education Bulletin* (Salisbury), 1967, *1*(1), pp. 3-7.

University College of Ghana. *Development of the Institute of Education,* 1960.

University of Ibadan. *Institute of Education – Draft Development Plan, 1961-1970,* 1960.

Verhaegen, Paul, and Laroche. "Some Methodological Considerations Concerning the Study of Aptitudes and the Elaboration of Psychological Tests for African Natives." *Journal of Social Psychology,* 1958, *47,* pp. 249-256.

White, Mary Alice. "Pupils' Perceptions of the School as a System: A Report of an Exploratory Study among Uganda Pupils." In *Child Growth and Development Projects,* National Institute of Education, Makerere University College, Kampala, Uganda, 1967.

Whiting, Beatrice, and Whiting, John. *Task Assignment and Personality: A Consideration of Herding on Boys.* Paper presented at the East African Social Science Conference, Dar es Salaam, Tanzania, January, 1968.

Wickert, Frederic (ed.). *Readings in African Psychology from French Language Sources.* African Studies Center, Michigan State University, 1967.

Yates, B. A. "Bibliography on Special Problems in Education in Tropical Africa." *Comparative Education Review,* 1964, *8,* pp. 307-319.

Afterword

When Judith Evans asked me to write an afterword to her annotated bibliography of studies on the behavior of children in Africa South of the Sahara, I was both flattered and pleased; flattered because I can think of others who might do the job better, and pleased because it gives me the opportunity to carry her book forward by suggesting areas for further research. In this, I am concerned not so much with reviewing the material in this book, as using it as a stimulus for further enquiry. Finally, as one who has also compiled a bibliography on human behavior in Africa, I think I can understand with some sympathy the problems involved in selecting and editing the material she has presented in her book.

1. Belief Systems

The book appropriately began with an attempt to summarize the strands of thinking that run through the fabric of African life. One of the few unities in Africa, with its wide differences in human ecology, language, and custom, seems to be of logic and metaphysics about the world and the relationships between events and people in the world.

The African world view is best seen as a system of causation that is consistent and logical, and conveyed in African languages in ways that languages of Indo-European origin would find difficult to express adequately. Studies of oral transmission of belief systems in observances and omens indicate that early verbal classification of the environment implies two major learning tasks which can be assumed from analyzing the content of the observances and omens. The knowledge implied in the observances is of two kinds: first, a detailed and specific knowledge of the functions of objects, animals, and plant life; second, a knowledge of the forces of these objects and their potential for social disruption through human or ancestral intervention in the web of causation.

The application of this research into African beliefs is straightforward. Concept formation in young children, for example, may be highly language specific, tied closely to the immediate environment, and is probably subject to considerable affective and emotional association because of the coexistence of a highly complex set of rules governing behavior toward objects in the environment. It seems that African psychologists could well find that experiments and concept formation with young children would vary according to whether the language used was indigenous or western. Second, the objects or symbols used for concept formation experiments would not just have to be familiar to the subjects, they would have to be incapable of disturbing the causal "field." Indeed, getting a clinically neutral set of objects, or representation of them, would be an interesting experiment in itself. It is not, incidentally, difficult to predict that the most everyday and commonplace objects symbolized in the local language might produce exceptional latencies of response in word-association tests because of their affective links with the belief system.

In short, the studies of *Ntu** (metaphysics and assumptions) and *Nommo* (practical exercise of spiritual force through the words and acts of men) are prerequisites for students of pure or applied psychology in Africa. Without awareness of and sensitivity to these belief systems built into the design, experimental work with children must inevitably appear clumsy and inhibiting to the African observer.

If one were to attempt a general hypothesis based on the study of belief systems, it would be that individual differences in personality and ability are very much a function of group-referent behavior – the more so because of the power of the belief systems. Moreover, the oral nature of much of the transmission of these beliefs makes common motivational themes of an archetypal nature a plausible hypothesis. The Jungian "racial unconscious" is not implied in this statement, of course, but tribally closed environments and oral traditions are key prerequisites for a socially inherited referent system for the development of personality.

2. Intelligence and Ability .

That the author gave early attention in her text to the problem of abilities and their measurement, is testimony to the lasting fascination of psychologists with the problem of assessing man's potential, either in relation to his peers within cultures or as a member of an ethnic group. The work in Africa has a history, and I now offer some comments about the development of the field of enquiry, together with a personal theoretical statement.

The early work of Fick (1939) and its refutation by Biesheuvel (1943) was really bound up with controversy over the *levels* of skills acquired by two different ethnic groups. The scientific point at issue, however, is not whether different ethnic groups attain different levels of competence in an array of skills valued by any society, but whether the concept of intelligence – as it may most commonly be derived from a study of intelligence test items used in western societies, or from a theoretical standpoint based on factor analysis of tests – is sufficient to (a) encompass the *kinds* of skills actually learned in

---

* Jahn's terms (in *Muntu: A Study of Neo-African Culture,* London: Faber, 1961) are used here for convenience.

Africa and (b) recognize the use to which early learned knowledge, passed on orally, is put. The works of Fick and Biesheuvel, indeed, at that stage were heavily influenced by Burt's hierarchical system, which related together certain groups of socially valued intellectual skills that were assumed to be high in the hierarchy of transferable abilities.

Although one of Biesheuvel's later works (1952) clearly recognized that there were unique aspects of learning in an African environment that could be regarded as "intelligent" behavior, the implication of this for theories of intelligence received little attention until recently. Logical analysis of the word "intelligent" reveals that it belongs to a family of value words and that its correct logical use is somewhat like that of "good" or "bad." If one weds this logical approach to the psychological viewpoint of Ferguson (1954, 1956) — that abilities are clusters of over-learned skills which are more or less correlated depending on their specificity — then it becomes clear that learned skills will vary within and between societies, depending on the value placed on them. An over-learned skill in one society may be only partially learned in another. What may be specific in one society may be part of a highly correlated group of skills in the next. One might thus define intelligent behavior as that which is learned, socially valued, purposeful, and commendable.

From this standpoint one can see that the transfer of educational systems from western Europe to other nations in the colonial era brought certain groups of skills that, initially, because of opposition in thought and value systems between indigenous people and missionaries, were resisted rather than sought for. Nowadays, of course, education is highly prized, indicating a shift in values. The successful adaptation of man to the requirements of literacy, numeracy, verbal and aural comprehension, and spatial and mechanical conceptualizations can be seen in the way in which tests of educational and cognitive abilities dependent on continuous education relate together when they are subjected to factor analysis. A review of factor analytic studies carried out cross-culturally in Africa (Macdonald, 1944-45; Beisheuvel, 1954; Irvine, 1964, 1966, 1969a), shows that cognitive tests will group themselves together to indicate clusters of relatively stable skills. These results can be explained by the relative homogeneity of skills learned in the schools of developing nations (heavily verbal, using English as a second language) and by the relative homogeneity of educational methods that are themselves a function of overcrowding and low levels of initial teacher training. Also, one must assume that there are individual differences in the capacity to learn, a capacity that doubtless depends on neurological fitness, and that interacts in much the same way with the same classes of stimuli across cultures.

Interesting as the similarity of test inter-correlations is across cultures, even more interesting is the lack of similarity in the effects of measures of the indigenous environment on the acquisition of cognitive skills. One of the few environmental constants across cultures is the learning situation in school. In this respect, individual differences among teachers in Africa produce greater effects than either individual differences among children or differences in family circumstances (Irvine, 1966). Moreover, Vernon's work (1969) with many cultures shows that the same variable measured in the same way in different cultures (e.g., male-female dominance in the family) has different correlations with factor scores presumed to represent the same abilities. One possible explanation for the differential action of environmental variables on cognitive variables seems to be the role of the society's value system in determining which skills shall be over-learned to the point that environmental influences are redundant. When this happens, test scores then reflect fairly pure measures of individual differences in ability to learn such skills. When there is variation on the value placed on skills, the environmental variables are correlated with skill acquisitions, provided that school standards are sufficiently homogeneous.

There are, of course, many skills learned by the African child of pre-school age. Among them are listening; learning the different language codes appropriate to parents, grandparents, and peers; and learning rules of observance and avoidance, particularly in village situations. They are learned because they are highly valued, and indicate that some of the earliest learning for African children is concerned with a system of causation that is teleological, implies concept development within the logic of such a system, and fulfills a distinct social function.

The most compelling feature of the analysis presented so far is the possibility of the development, side by side in highly educated African students, of two independent systems of causation. African children, as they learn the language of their parents and kinfolk, learn with it an indigneous concept system that exerts social control, thus compelling the development of certain cognitive skills within its logic. School systems introduce knowledge, the function of which is quite different and, in many instances, cannot be conveyed accurately in the vernacular.

One way to reconcile the problems posed by the coexistence of sets of congnitive skills with functions that reflect different ideologies, is to posit different modes of thought, related in hypothetical ways. The initial learning within the parental value system and language code can be considered *primary*. It would exert affective and stylistic control over cognitive functions. Learning in school situations would, when it occurs largely through a second language, be termed *secondary*.* When such learning conflicts with

---

* It seems possible to extend this theory to sub-groups within any society. Bernstein's formulation of restricted and elaborated codes of language can be seen within this context.

the ideology of the primary mode, then the first system would have to be successfully inhibited before learning could take place.

3. Development

(a) Nutritional Problems. In nutrition studies, the effect of kwashiorkor on cognitive functions has been investigated over a wide area and for some years. Although protein and vitamin deficiency must be held to be endemic in large sections of the African population, little of a substantive nature has emerged. If systematic developmental studies of the effects of these deficiencies are contemplated, then it seems likely that whole communities will be requested to participate in order to exert sufficient control over experimental conditions. If this is not feasible on the grounds of cost, then animal experiments might be necessary: but then one is faced with the perennial problem of comparability of physiology and cognitive process. However, the challenge is there for a study, involving FAO, WHO, UNICEF, and other international agencies, in which psychologists can play a major role.

Finally, if one were to pinpoint a primary goal in the physiological field, it would be the establishment of carefully constructed normative studies in use in medical and social welfare programs.

(b) Normal Development. The bibliography shows this area to be surprisingly well-documented. There is a sizeable, and extremely important, amount of systematic work on child health, largely based in east Africa, and centered on the efforts of Jellife and his co-workers. There have also been general accounts of child rearing on both sides of the continent, evidenced by the writing of Raum, Barrington-Kaye, Reed, and E. B. Castle. Developmental and "readiness" schedules, albeit western culture-centered, have been applied, and there are several studies of parent-child relationships, notably by Geber and Knapen, in infant psychomotor development. There is still, however, a lack of measuring instruments that show awareness of the content and purpose of early concept development in African villages. It seems likely, though, that such measures are only a short distance away.

The second prerequisite to studies in the developmental area appears to be a systematic examination of environmental variation within Africa itself. Environment includes physical surroundings, early language input, and affective climate. The work of Berry (1966) shows that different environments can produce the same perceptual organization of skills (Eskimo vs. Scottish Hebrides children) and different as well (Eskimo vs. Temne). For example, one might have to control for major language groups, urban and rural dwellers, tropical rain forest, savannah and arid regions, and matrilineal and patrilineal characteristics. The continent offers a rich variety of conditions for systematic variation of environmental variables.

In retrospect, two others areas of concern to social anthropologists seem relatively untouched. These are adolescence – where some societies mark the transition to adulthood ceremonially and some do not – and aging – where life expectancy is still relatively short. Both seem worthy of investigation in order to test the many assumptions that characterize thinking about problems associated with these developmental stages.

(c) Social Forces. The major conclusion that can be drawn from studying the material of social influences on development is that there is a problem is translating the work done on groups into individual differences. One would like, for example, to have a great deal of the original field interview data collected by sociologists in order to discern the range of individual variation in the actions often ascribed to families, whole villages, or groups in cities. One would also like to be able to test the many acute and intuitive hypotheses put forward by sociologists about the nature of social interactions and the factors that control them. These studies contain much sociological work of relevance to the psychologist, since they cover the same ground from a different viewpoint and from a different methodology.

This apart, work in social psychology done with questionnaires and attitude inventories is still very culture-bound. From experience with responses to written material presented to African students, one concludes that acquiescence and response-styles may account for a great deal of variance in replies. This may be overcome by seeking a new focus for the construction of inventories based on a deeper understanding of the forces that govern behavior toward peers, kin, and ancestors. The earlier works of Biesheuvel (1958, 1959) have only recently been extended by Dawson (1967). These writers are primarily concerned with the dimension traditionalism vs. westernism or modernism. There still remains the need for a clearer study of what traditionalism is or means for the socialization of the individual.

Finally, the whole question of cross-cultural comparison of data becomes a very much more open one when one realizes that the differences between English and French, as a medium of communication of feelings, are much less than those between either language and the local vernacular. One may be missing the whole area of affect by writing questions for attitude inventories in English and/or French. Hence, comparison may be limited to a restricted domain of behaviors; one can perhaps conjecture what happens when sophisticated factorial or scaling techniques are applied to domains that are restricted for one population but may be global for another.

4. Perception

In this area the major interest has been in visual perception and illusions. This material has been admirably synthesized by Segall, Campbell, and Herskovits (1966) and, unlike a great deal of research in Africa, has a history and the beginnings of a systematic theory. Nevertheless, the field shows large gaps; in aural perception, for example, it has been suggested that rhythmic encoding may be over-learned in many African areas. The one significant experiment by Harmon (1963) on aural perception of phoneme pairs, however, does not appear to indicate acute discrimination. In general, experiments have not been conducted in situations where subjects could be observed responding to stimuli under the conditions of the immediate environment. Paper and pencil conventions are little understood by the vast majority of respondents, while experiments involving apparatus under various degrees of illumination may have affective influences on illiterate and even literate African subjects about which we can only surmise.

As yet no psychologist has investigated the claim often made by African collegues and students that perception of markings in domestic animals, birds, leaves, and plants occurs in fine detail at an early age. Those who have witnessed girls in Northern Nigeria or in Ghana play a game in which the dance steps of the leader, at the center of a ring of girls, are studied by those on the outside in an attempt to match them, will realize that if the leader has only 10 variations she has factorial 10 permutations of steps which the players on the outside ring must perceive, learn, and predict. To the western eye, unaided by a high-speed camera, the task is all but impossible, yet the game is played by girls of all ages.

One fruitful line of investigation, then, seems to rest in an attempt to free perceptual experiments from some of our own conventions in order to get close to individual differences unclouded by cognitive processes that intrude through coping with cultural barriers in the experiment. Other areas in need of systematic work involve reaction times and color vision, particularly the relationship among color discrimination, color coding in language, and the affective meaning of color words. For experimenters with an interest in genetics, systematic studies on the incidence of color blindness in various regions of Africa would be an excellent field.

5. Educational Psychology.

In a sense, Africa South of the Sahara is one of the most intensively "surveyed" areas of the world. This statement tells us a great deal about psychological research in education. The great majority of it has dealt with surveys, since educational psychologists have been laying the groundwork for other research. Topics that have been given attention in an empirical way include wastage, aspirations, girls' education, and selection to secondary school. These are concerned with the quantity and purpose of education in Africa. Teaching methods and experimental procedures have hardly been touched upon, simply because universal education is not a reality. Thus, methodological studies have a low priority: it is clear that only by finding the most suitable conditions for learning in large groups – given teachers with minimal qualifications – will the goal of universal primary education be realized. This seems to be the most outstanding problem of action research in Africa, and one that encompasses learning, motivation, group behavior, and teacher education. Its solution will not be found by one man, but by an interdisciplinary team. Indeed, the need for interdisciplinary cooperation is marked in almost every area surveyed in this book.

Hence, I commend this book to the student of human behavior in Africa. The challenge to the assumptions of Western theories of psychology is there for those patient and interested enough to meet it. There is little doubt that the student of Africa, whatever his field, may learn something from this book, while the social scientist can hardly avoid it if he is to be aware of a whole new field of study that even now demands serious recognition as an academic discipline in its own right.

S. H. Irvine
University of Western Ontario

BIBLIOGRAPHY

Berry, J. W. "Ecology, Perceptual Development and the Müller-Lyer Illusion." *British Journal of Psychology,* 1968, *59,* pp. 205-210.

Biesheuvel, S. *African Intelligence.* Johannesburg: South African Institute of Race Relations, 1943.

———. "The Study of African Ability, I and II." *African Studies,* 1952, *II,* pp. 45-57 and 105-117.

———. "The Measurement of Occupational Aptitudes in a Multiracial Society." *Occupational Psychology,* 1954, *28,* pp. 189-196.

Dawson, J. L. M. "Cultural and Physiological Influences Upon Spatial-Perceptual Processes in West Africa: I and II." *International Journal of Psychology,* 1967, *2,* pp. 115-128 and 171-185.

Ferguson, G. A. "On Learning and Human Ability." *Canadian Journal of Psychology,* 1954, *8,* pp. 95-112.

———. "On Transfer and the Abilities of Man." *Canadian Journal of Psychology,* 1956, *10,* pp. 121-131.

Fick, M. L. *The Educability of the South African Native.* South African Council for Educational Research, 1939.

Guthrie, G. H. "Structure of Abilities in a Non-Western Culture." *Journal of Educational Psychology,* 1963, *2,* pp. 94-103.

Harmon, R. J. "An Experiment in Testing Aural Perception in English." *Rhodes-Livingstone Journal,* 1963, *34,* pp. 36-43.

Irvine, S. H. "Ability Testing in English-Speaking Africa – An Overview of Comparative and Predictive Studies." *Rhodes-Livingtone Journal,* 1964, *34,* pp. 44-55.

———. "Towards a Rationale for Testing Attainments and Abilities in Africa." *British Journal of Educational Psychology,* 1966, *36,* pp. 24-32.

————. "Contributions of Ability and Attainment Testing in Africa to a General Theory of Intellect." *Journal of Bio-Sociological Science,* 1969a, Supplement (1), pp. 91-102.

————. "Examination and the Economy: A Study in Africa." In *World Yearbook of Education.* London: Evans Brothers, 1969b.

————. "Degrees and Dimensions of Social Interaction in Tribal Groupings: A Sociometric Study." *International Journal of Psychology,* 1969c, *4*, pp. 27-38.

Macdonald, A. *Selection of African Personnel.* Reports on the Work of the Selection of Personnel Technical and Research Unit, Middle East Force. Ministry of Defence Archives, London, 1944-5.

Segall, M. H., Campbell, D. T., and Herskovits, M. J. *The Influences of Culture on Visual Perception.* New York: Bobbs-Merrill, 1966.

Vernon, P. E. *Intelligence and Cultural Environment.* London: Methuen, 1969.